# Ancient Treasures

# BRIAN HAUGHTON

# ANCIENT TREASURES

*The Discovery of Lost Hoards,
Sunken Ships, Buried Vaults, and
Other Long-Forgotten Artifacts*

NEW PAGE BOOKS
A division of The Career Press, Inc.
Pompton Plains, NJ

ANCIENT TREASURES

Edited by Jodi Brandon
Typeset by Eileen Munson
Cover design by Joseph Sherman
Printed in the U.S.A.

To order this title, please call toll-free 1-800-CAREER-1 (NJ and Canada: 201-848-0310) to order using VISA or MasterCard, or for further information on books from Career Press.

The Career Press, Inc.
220 West Parkway, Unit 12
Pompton Plains, NJ 07444
www.careerpress.com
www.newpagebooks.com

Library of Congress Cataloging-in-Publication Data
Haughton, Brian, 1964-
  Ancient treasures : the discovery of lost hoards, sunken ships, buried vaults, and other long-forgotten artifacts / by Brian Haughton.
    pages cm
  Includes bibliographical references and index.
  ISBN 978-1-60163-249-4 -- ISBN 978-1-60163-548-8 (ebook) 1. Treasure troves--Anecdotes 2. Antiquities--Anecdotes. 3. Coin hoards--Anecdotes. 4. Hoards, Prehistoric--Anedotes. I. Title.

G525.H3226 2013
622'.19--dc23

2013012532

For Marion Haughton

## Acknowledgments

Thanks to my agent Lisa Hagan, of Paraview, and my family for putting up with me during the writing of this book.

# CONTENTS

"Treasure" can take many forms. It might be an ancient chest brimming with gold and silver objects, a romantic image of something almost mystical hidden away and forgotten in bygone times, even a legal term defined by law to denote certain types of artifacts dug up from the ground. The 1997 Treasure Act in the UK, gives a number of different types of find that qualify as treasure, including:

> Any metallic object, other than a coin, provided that at least 10 per cent by weight of metal is precious metal (that is, gold or silver) and that it is at least 300 years old when found. If the object is of prehistoric date it will be Treasure provided any part of it is precious metal.... All coins from the same find provided they are at least 300 years old when found.... Only the following groups of coins will normally be regarded as coming from the same find: hoards that have been deliberately hidden...smaller groups of coins, such as the contents of purses, that may been dropped or lost...votive or ritual deposits.[1]

But is the human fascination with such treasure purely a desire for wealth, or has it more to do with the romantic appeal of

I N T R O D U C T I O N

tales of lost ancient artifacts? It is certainly true that the stories behind the loss and recovery of a number of ancient treasures, like the Sevso Treasure and the Amber Room, for example, read like edge-of-the-seat fiction, somewhere between Indiana Jones and James Bond. But treasure need not always be in the form of gold and silver jewelry, weaponry or coins, as the chapter on the incredible cache of mummies from Deir el-Bahri, on the west bank of the Nile, opposite the city of Luxor, in Egypt, shows. The main connection between the treasures discussed in this work is that each has a story. From the riches of Tutankhamun's tomb in Egypt's Valley of the Kings, to the northern European hoards of the Vikings, from ancient Chinese Treasure Ships to Nazi lootings during WWII, every treasure has a fascinating tale to tell. Such stories can shed much-needed light on the ancient cultures that originally deposited the artifacts; or, if the objects were looted from their original context, it may be the often-labyrinthine journeys of the treasures after their discovery in modern times that provide us with the astonishing narrative. In this way the ancient and the modern combine to create a unique picture of the objects that goes beyond archaeology and history.

Two chapters in this book deal with a favorite theme of treasure hunting tales: shipwrecks. The rich New World plunder of the Spanish treasure fleets of the 16th to 18th centuries has been the target of elaborate salvage attempts by modern treasure hunters, mainly off the Florida coast, whereas the remains of Admiral Zheng He's huge Chinese treasure ships of the 15th century and their cargoes have been far more difficult to track down. The world of fake ancient artifacts is covered in another section of this work, which shows that as long as there are people rich enough and greedy enough to be fooled by appearance, often spectacularly so, as in the case of the Chiemsee Cauldron, then the trade in fake antiquities will continue to flourish.

A recurring theme in *Ancient Treasures* is looted treasure, and the way it more often than not finds its way to many of the world's greatest museums, which have knowingly accepted such illegally excavated treasure hoards. There is a stark contrast between the European and North American leisure pursuit of treasure hunting, and the activities of looters in poor countries, such as some nations in Africa, Asia, Latin America, and the Middle East, which are rich in archaeological remains. (See the chapters on the Lydian Hoard and the Morgantina Treasure.) Looting is a way of life for some villagers in these areas, though they often receive as little as 1 percent of the actual value of the objects they recover, the rest going to middlemen and dealers. A country's archaeological sites and museums are always most at risk of looting during times of war and political upheaval, and it has been estimated that between 3,000 and 7,000 objects are still missing from the Iraq Museum, which was looted in April 2003.

Archaeological looting, however, is not confined to poorer countries. In Britain, archaeological sites are still under threat from illegal metal detecting, mostly done at night by people rather romantically nicknamed "nighthawks." ("Thieves" would be a more apt description.) A 1988 congressional report on vandalism and looting in the archaeologically rich Four Corners region of the United States (where the boundaries of New Mexico, Arizona, Utah, and Colorado meet) stated that up to 90 percent of known Native American archaeological sites in the region had been vandalized. In an article in *The Arizona Republic* ("Stolen Artifacts Shatter Ancient Culture," November 12, 2006), Dennis Wagner reported that an estimated 80 percent of the ancient archaeological sites in the United States have been plundered. The recent phenomenon of e-trading in illicit antiquities has exacerbated the problem of looting. As Karen Olsen Bruhns says in an online article, "The past is being bulldozed out of the ground and being sold on-line."[2] Unfortunately, the fact is that as long as the demand is there (which it certainly is: The illicit market is measured in billions of dollars per year), the looting of archaeological sites and the black market for antiquities will continue.

There is often a great deal of myth and folklore surrounding treasure; indeed, some so-called treasures are probably more mythical than real (for example, the Treasure of the Knights Templar, the Ark of the Covenant, Yamashita's gold, the gold of El Dorado). It is interesting that the most common folklore theme connected with treasures is that of some type of curse or retribution for disturbing an antiquity, as if to suggest that no one should ever be allowed to get something for nothing. The infamous Curse of Tutankhamun is examined in the chapter on Tutankhamun's Treasure, but there are a number of other examples from the annals of folklore.

The infamous Captain Kidd (d. May 1701) is alleged to have buried treasure on Charles Island, off the coast of Milford, Connecticut, in Long Island Sound, and put a death curse on anyone who attempted to retrieve it. When a man named Paul Parry found a gold image (in some versions a cross) 5 inches long in the Bronze Age cairn on Carnedd y Ddelw, a summit in the Carneddau Mountains in north Wales, in 1812, he took it home, but his house immediately became haunted so he threw the object away. Interestingly, the name of this burial site translates as "cairn of the idol." There were more serious consequences for a laborer who, some years before 1630, attempted to retrieve an earthen pot of treasure from Broken Barrow mound, a Bronze Age burial mound near Challacombe in Devon, in the west of England. As soon as he grabbed hold of the pot he heard the noise of thundering horses' hooves, but when he turned around there was nothing to be seen. The man left without the treasure but soon afterward lost both his sight and hearing, and in less than three months he died. In 1923 or 1924 the tenant of Claughbane farm, near Ramsey, in the north of the Isle of Man (an island in the Irish Sea between Great Britain and Ireland), and some of his workers dug into a burial mound looking for treasure. Within a couple of months the men had caught pneumonia and all but one subsequently died.

However, in folklore terms, it was more usual for excavations at ancient sites to be either stopped or followed by terrible thunderstorms, as at Burley Camp, an iron age hillfort in Devon; the Bronze Age burial mound at Carnedd Cerrig, Hirnant, Powys, mid-Wales; and another Bronze Age burial mound at Wood Barrow on the Devon/Somerset border. Such folkloric thunderstorms have the whiff of divine punishment about them, assumingly meted out for breaking into a sacred place. One of the many legends concerning the throwing of treasure into the River Ogmore in South Wales may be linked with ancient ritual deposits in watery places. The story involves a girl who was going to a well for water near the ruins of an ancient house in Bryncethin, near Bridgend, South Wales, when the place was suddenly hit by forked lightening. The next day when she visited the well the same thing happened. On the third occasion the girl met with the ghost of a lady dressed in antique clothes wandering among the wild rose bushes. When the girl summoned the courage to talk to the apparition, she was told to go to the ruined house and remove a hoard of coins and precious stones contained in a bag hidden underneath the hearthstone. When the girl had retrieved the treasure she was instructed by the lady to throw it into the River Ogmore, after which she never saw the apparition again.

A number of stories in this book examine how treasures, in the form of hoards, are hidden during times of war and catastrophe, such as at ancient Pompeii, and much more recently during the war in Afghanistan. This theme is linked to the often fabulously wealthy Roman and Viking hoards buried in the ground for safekeeping when their civilizations were beginning to crumble, only to be unearthed centuries later by humble metal detectorists. It must be noted that it is often not possible to tell why and by whom a hoard was deposited in the ground; there were probably a wide variety of reasons, some of which would perhaps be beyond our understanding. Although hoards often may have been buried for safekeeping, the preponderance of many of them close to rivers, streams, and wells (for example, at Bath, at the River Thames at London Bridge, and at Llyn Fawr, a lake in the Cynon Valley, South Wales), and the massive nature of some deposits (such as the Frome hoard of 52,500 Roman coins, from Somerset in the West of England) do suggest a ritual explanation for some examples. Apart from such votive hoards, other types of caches include: merchant's hoards of newly made objects ready for distribution; founder's hoards of broken or scrap metal objects, ingots, casting waste, and sometimes complete objects, collected together for recycling; hoards of loot collected from battle and raiding; and dealer's hoards, objects of various dates and styles gathered together by antique collectors or dealers, many of which were not originally discovered together.

The appeal and excitement of ancient treasure and the stories connected with it is undeniable. Recent widely publicized discoveries of ancient treasure hoards such as the Staffordshire Anglo Saxon hoard, valued at £3.2 million in 2009 (see the chapter on this hoard), the Frome hoard of 2010, and the magnificent hoard of 50,000 silver and Bronze Iron Age Celtic coins discovered in June 2012 on the island of Jersey, just off the coast of Normandy, France, have contributed to the dramatic rise in the popularity of treasure hunting and metal detecting throughout the last decade or so. Further afield the 1,800-year-old cache of 140 gold and silver coins and gold jewelry, from the area of Kiryat Gat, in southern Israel, and the exquisite 2,400-year-old hoard of Thracian gold from a tomb in Sveshtari, Bulgaria, both discovered in 2012, show that fantastic discoveries are still being made, and our knowledge of the ancient world is continually being added to.

## The Deir el-Bahri
## Mummy Cache

*B*etween 1875 and 1881 a number of objects belonging to ancient pharaonic tombs, including figures bearing royal names from the 21st Dynasty and a papyrus belonging to Queen Nedjmet (Late 20th Dynasty, c1087– 1080 BC), appeared for sale on the antiquities market in Egypt and also made their way into private collections abroad. Concerned about the origin of these artifacts, Gaston Maspero, director of the Egyptian Antiquities Service, decided to investigate. Maspero's inquiries eventually led him to the village of Qurnah on the West Bank of the River Nile opposite the modern city of Luxor. Here Maspero was taken to the Abdou el-Rassul family, who had some years previously discovered a royal tomb in the area and had been systematically looting it ever since. Information from the family led Maspero to the nearby temple and tomb complex of Deir el-Bahri, and the discovery and excavation of the tomb (known romantically as either Tomb DB320 or TT320) with spectacular results. The tomb revealed an incredible cache of more than 40 royal mummies, including those of Tuthmosis I and his son Ramses II. A few years later

CHAPTER

1

another cache, this time of 153 mummies of high priests, was found in another tomb at the site, and in March 1898, a further cache of royal mummies was discovered in the neighboring Valley of the Kings. Why had these mummies been removed from their individual tombs and gathered together in one place, and who had put them there?

Deir el-Bahri (Arabic for "the Northern Monastery") is a complex of mortuary temples and tombs located on the west bank of the Nile, opposite the city of Luxor, not too far from the entrance to the Valley of the Kings. The first monument constructed on the site was the mortuary complex of 11th Dynasty pharaoh Mentuhotep II, who ruled from 2008 to 1957 BC. Eighteenth Dynasty pharaoh Amenhotep I (who reigned from 1526 to 1506 BC), the first king of Egypt to separate his mortuary temple from his tomb, built a temple at Deir el-Bahri that was later torn down by Queen Hatshepsut (1508–1458 BC), the fifth pharaoh of the 18th Dynasty. Over the ruins of Amenhotep's temple Hatshepsut built her own mortuary temple (partly based on that of Mentuhotep II) named Djeser-Djeseru ("Holy of Holies"), a magnificent colonnaded structure built into a cliff face, which is now the best preserved and most impressive temple at the site. It was in a tomb in a niche hidden in the cliffs behind these temples that the Deir el-Bahri cache of royal mummies was found.

Although Gaston Maspero was not alerted to the presence of the mummy cache until 1881, there is a possibility that two of three brothers from the Abdou el-Rassul family (Ahmed, Hussein, and Mohammed) had discovered the mummies as early as 1860. When questioned by the authorities, the brothers at first refused to admit to the thefts, but later, after the arrest and torture of his brothers, Mohammed el-Rassul, the eldest of the three, admitted the nature of their activities and led Emile Brugsch, Maspero's assistant, to the site of the mummy cache. Ahmed el-Rassul, who had been working as a guide and dealer, also told the story of how he had found the cache in 1871 (1875 in some versions of the tale) while searching for a lost goat among the cliffs around Deir el-Bahri. Ahmed apparently found that his goat had fallen down one of the numerous vertical tomb shafts that peppered the cliffs. Unwilling to lose the animal, Ahmed clambered down the dark shaft after it until he reached a corridor. There he lit a candle and was astounded to discover that he was surrounded by huge wooden coffins piled on top of one another, with various funerary articles such as shabtis (small funerary figurines), canopic jars, and funerary papyri scattered all around. Since this discovery, the Abdou el-Rassul family had been living well by looting artifacts from the tomb and selling them off a few at a time.

This story is strangely reminiscent of the discovery of the Dead Sea Scrolls in 1947 by Bedouin goat-herders while searching the cliffs along Wadi Qumran near the Dead Sea for a lost goat. It is also just as false. What actually happened was that in 1871 the el-Rassul brothers, who by that time were already involved in looting and selling artifacts, discovered the tomb shaft by accident. Having entered the tomb and realizing its vast wealth, the brothers decided on a method of keeping other tomb-robbers away from their find. Exploiting the Arabic myth of the *afrit,* an enormous winged fire-creature said to inhabit underground ruins, the brothers told other villagers that there was a terrible odor coming from the newly discovered tomb, proof that there was an afrit living inside it. Indeed, when villagers ventured near the shaft there was no mistaking the rank odor emanating from the tomb. Was this proof of the reality of the afrit? Not exactly. What the brothers had actually done was to kill a donkey and throw its corpse into the tomb, natural decay doing the rest.

When Mohammed el-Rassul led Emile Brugsch and officials from the Egyptian Antiquities Service to the tomb, they found that, although many of the funerary goods were long gone and the gold sarcophagi had been melted down, the royal mummies themselves appeared to be intact. With the threat of further looting by local villagers, a dangerous reality now that the location of the tomb was known, the Antiquities Service decided to act quickly. Within five days of its official discovery Brugsch had organized the excavation of the tomb and, with the help of 300 workers, had the remarkable mummies and more than 6,000 artifacts removed and shipped down the Nile to the Egyptian Museum in Cairo. Unfortunately, due to time limitations, Brugsch had not taken a single photograph of the mummies or funerary goods in situ, nor had he drawn up a precise plan of the tomb or made a list of the finds.

Primarily because of his inside knowledge of the local antiquities black market, Mohammed el-Rassul was subsequently given a job as foreman for the Egyptian Antiquities Society. This appointment was to pay off in a big way when in 1891 Mohammed led one of the Society's inspectors to another tomb at Deir el-Bahri (called Bab el Gasus), which contained the mummies of 160 high priests of Amun. However, the Society soon discovered that el-Rassul had known about this cache for some time before he revealed the location to the authorities, and he was subsequently fired from his job. A further cache of mummies was discovered in March 1898, this time in the nearby Valley of the Kings, by French archaeologist Victor Loret. Known as KV35, this tomb belonged to Amenhotep II (who reigned from 1427 to 1401 BC) but also contained a number of other corpses scattered around and a few interred in side chambers of the tomb. There were 13 mummies in all, most of them belonging to Egyptian royalty. Some of these were without coffins and had been stripped of their bandages. The mummies in the side chamber all had a large hole in their skulls, and their breasts had been split open, the result of the activities of tomb-robbers in a hurry to remove jewelry and amulets from the bandages.

On November 24, 1901, the night guards in the Valley of the Kings claimed that they were overpowered by more than a dozen attackers who then proceeded to rifle the contents of KV35. Amenhotep II's mummy was cut open and his amulets and jewels stolen, the body removed from the sarcophagus and damaged in the process. The attack was investigated by the chief inspector of Antiquities for Upper Egypt, Howard Carter (of future Tutankhamun fame), who believed that the robbery had been an "inside job" and, after examining footprints at the site, concluded that there had not been more than one or two people in the tomb.

Carter's chief suspect in the looting of KV35 was none other than our old friend Mohamed el-Rassul, though the case against him was dropped due to insufficient evidence. Carter subsequently resigned from the Antiquities Service in 1903.

Of all the mummy caches, Tomb DB320 has probably the most remarkable collection of Egyptian royalty. Included in the cache were mummies of Ramses II and III; Amenhotep I; Tuthmosis I, II, and III; Seti I; Ahmose I; and Pinudjem I and II. It is believed that the tomb itself was the family vault of the Theban high priest Pinudjem II, though this is by no means certain. Examination of the corpses from the tomb by British-Australian anatomist and anthropologist Grafton Elliot Smith (the results of which

he published in detail in his 1912 *Catalogue of the Royal Mummies*) provides some fascinating details about the Egyptian rulers. Smith's examination of the body of Tuthmosis II (who ruled 1518–1504 BC and who was married to his half-sister Hatshepsut) revealed that the ruler, like all the Tuthmosids, had a noticeable over-bite and was just 5' 6" in height. Smith also noted that Tuthmosis II was virtually bald and that the skin of his face was wrinkled, suggesting that the king was over 30 when he died, though what he died of is a mystery, as no obvious cause of death could be found.

*1.1. Tuthmosis III basalt statue in Luxor Museum. Courtesy of Wikipedia.*

Smith's examination of the body of Seti I, who ruled 1291–1278 BC and was known for building the incredible 80-feet-high Hypostyle Hall at Karnak, revealed that it was the best preserved of all mummies from Tomb DB320, and that the ruler had died in his 60s, perhaps from complications resulting from a chronic ear infection.

The mummy cache from Tomb KV35 included the mummies of Thutmose IV; Amenhotep III; Ramses IV, V, and VI; and Seti II. There were also two female mummies, one of which is the so-called "Elder Lady," which, after DNA testing as part of the *King Tutankhamun Family Project* (September 2007 to October 2009), was revealed in 2010 to be that of Queen Tye (c1398–1338 BC). Queen Tye was the Great Royal Wife of the pharaoh Amenhotep III and was also Tutankhamun's grandmother. The other female mummy in the cache was given the title the "Younger Lady," and Grafton Elliot Smith's examinations revealed her to have been 5' 2" in height, and no older than 25 at the time of her death. Smith also noted significant damage to the mummy, which was thought to have been caused by ancient tomb-robbers. However, the large wound in the left side of the mummy's mouth and cheek is now believed to have been inflicted prior to death and to have been a lethal injury, indicating that the lady was in fact murdered. In 2003 British Egyptologist Dr. Joann Fletcher controversially claimed that the Younger Lady was none other than Nefertiti (c1370–c1330 BC) the Great Royal Wife of the pharaoh Akhenaten. However, this theory was rejected by most Egyptologists, including Dr. Zahi Hawass, Egyptologist and former Egyptian Minister of State for Antiquities Affairs, who initially believed that the mummy was that of a man. However, DNA testing of the Younger Lady during the *King Tutankhamun Family Project* revealed the mummy to be female, probably both the sister and wife of Akhenaten, and also the mother of Tutankhamun. Candidates for the identity of the Younger Lady include Akhenaten's second wife, Kiya; daughters of Amenhotep III, Nebetah or Beketaten; or Meritaten, daughter of Akhenaten and Nefertiti.

But why had large numbers of royal mummies been found collected together in these caches? Why were they not left in the splendor of their original private tombs? The story really begins with the decline of the New Kingdom after the assassination of Ramses III around 1156 BC. With the rise of new foreign powers, Egypt began losing its grip on its empire in Asia, then came droughts, famine, severe official corruption, and internal strife caused primarily by the increase in power of the priesthood of Amun at Thebes. Indeed the high priests wielded such political power and influence that they became essentially the rulers of Upper Egypt from 1080 to c943 BC. Two of these high priests were Pinedjem I and Pinedjem II. Pinedjem I controlled Middle and Upper Egypt from 1070 to 1032 BC, while at the same time Smendes, the founder of Egypt's 21st Dynasty, ruled over Lower Egypt. Pinedjem I's mummy was one of those found in the royal cache at Deir el-Bahri. Pinedjem II also ruled over the south of Egypt (from 990 to 976 BC), and his mummy along with those of his wives and a daughter were also discovered in Tomb DB320 at Deir el-Bahri.

During this chaotic time in Egypt's history the looting of royal tombs had increased to epidemic proportions. In an attempt to rescue the royal mummies from the sacrilege of tomb looting, it was the powerful high priests of Amun who organized the removal of the mummies from their original tombs in the Valley of the Kings to a more secure location in the cliffs around Deir el-Bahri. Before removing the mummies, both Pinudjem I and Pinudjem II identified and relabeled them, and also replaced some of the coffins that had grown weak with age. Text written in ink on some of the mummies and labels on a number of coffins show that the mummies were moved around more than once, traveling from tomb to tomb before arriving at their final resting places of tombs DB320 and KV35, and at Bab el Gasus. For example, text on the coffins of Ramses I, Seti I, and Ramses II shows that during the reign of Pinedjem I these coffins had been hidden in the tomb of the late-17th-Dynasty Queen Ahmose-Inhapi, daughter of the pharaoh Senakhtenre-Tao I (who reigned from around 1560 BC).

Queen Ahmose-Inhapi's mummy was found near the entrance of one of the corridors in Tomb DB320, with a linen label inscribed "The King's daughter and king's wife, Inhapi, may she live!" With the numerous reburials in various tombs, many of the rich grave goods that had originally accompanied the Egyptian royal dead disappeared. Although Gaston Maspero believed that New Kingdom tomb-robbers were probably responsible for looting these artifacts, modern Egyptologists are of the opinion that it was the Theban high priests themselves who appropriated most of the valuable funerary equipment, either for their own personal use or, more likely, to help bolster an increasingly unstable economy. Whatever happened to these valuable grave goods, it is clear that if the high priests of Amun had not responded to the threat of tomb-robbing in the way they did, our knowledge of pharaonic Egypt would be much the poorer.

## The Discovery of Tutankhamun's Treasure

The incredible discovery of Tutankhamun's tomb in the Valley of the Kings in 1922 captured the attention of the world and sparked an interest in ancient Egypt that still flourishes today. Not only did the 18-year-old Egyptian king become a household name, but the excavator of the tomb, Howard Carter, and his wealthy benefactor, Lord Carnarvon, achieved worldwide recognition for their discovery of Tutankhamun's rich treasures. The king's mummy and the astonishing finds from his tomb have provided us with vital information about how Egyptian pharaohs lived and died, as well as about religious beliefs in ancient Egypt. Carter's diaries, notes, and photographs, preserved at the Griffith Institute in Oxford[1], provide a fascinating and detailed insight into the 1922 excavations in the ancient Necropolis known as the Valley of the Kings, on the west bank of the Nile, opposite modern Luxor. Yet despite these records and the very public nature of the discovery, most of Carter's finds were never fully published, leaving unanswered questions about the tomb and its discovery. For example, how had Tutankhamun's tomb survived unplundered for more than 3,000 years when practically every other royal burial discovered from ancient times had been looted in some way? And what is the truth behind the so-called Curse of the Pharaohs, and why did it gain such currency?

*2.1. Burial chamber in Tutankhamun's tomb. Image by Mr. Arif Solak. Licensed under the Creative Commons Attribution-Share Alike 3.0 Unported license on Wikipedia.*

Tutankhamun was born in 1341 BC, the son of 18th Dynasty pharaoh Akhenaten, and ascended the throne probably in 1332/3 BC at the age of 8 or 9 upon the death of his father. Tutankhamun ("Living Image of Amun") ruled from his capital at Memphis, to the south of modern Cairo, and married his half-sister, Ankhesenpaaten. They had two children but both were stillborn. As such a young king it is probable that Tutankhamun's rule depended heavily on the advice from powerful officials like the vizier Ay and the general Horemheb, both of whom were to become pharaohs after Tutankhamun's death. As pharaoh, Tutankhamun's father, Akhenaten, had broken with religious tradition, sanctioning the worship of only one god, Aten, and rejecting all other gods. Akhenaten, known as the Heretic King, had also moved the Egyptian capital from the traditional Thebes (where modern Luxor now stands) to a new city in mid-Egypt named after himself and today known as el-Amarna. During his reign of about nine years Tutankhamun restored Egypt's traditional gods and their temples, including Amun, and brought the worship of Aten to an end. He also re-established Thebes as the religious capital of Egypt. When he was around 17 or 18 years old Tutankhamun died unexpectedly, probably as a result of malaria and an infected broken leg after a fall from his chariot. A recent theory regarding the king's death suggested by Hutan Ashrafian, a surgeon at Imperial College London, is that he suffered from a form of temporal lobe epilepsy and that his broken leg was caused by a seizure, which led to the fall.

After his death around 1323 BC, Tutankhamun was buried in a relatively small tomb in the Valley of the Kings. The size of his tomb may be due to the fact that his death was rather sudden, before there was time for the completion of a more imposing royal tomb; indeed it seems probable that Tutankhamun was buried in a tomb originally built for someone else, perhaps a court official. Carter's excavations of the tomb revealed three different sets of seals on the doorway, evidence that the doorways had been closed on three separate occasions. This indicated that thieves had entered there at least twice soon after the burial, and the disturbed nature of the tomb contents showed that they had made off with small valuable items such as jewelry. After Tutankhamun's tomb was sealed for the last time, debris from the construction of other tombs accumulated in front of it, and almost two centuries later workmen constructing the tomb of Ramses VI (who reigned 1145–1137 BC) built their huts over its entrance, thus concealing it from view and inadvertently protecting it from grave-robbers for more than 3,000 years, until the arrival of English archaeologist Howard Carter in the early 20th century.

Born in London, England, in 1873, Howard Carter first came to Egypt in 1891 as a 17-year-old artist hired by archaeologist Percy Newbury to help excavate and record artifacts from the

Middle Kingdom (c2030–1640 BC) tombs at Beni Hasan in Middle Egypt. Throughout the next eight years, Carter worked on various archaeological sites in Egypt including El-Amarna (under pioneer archaeologist Flinders Petrie), Thebes, and Deir el-Bahri (on the west bank of the Nile opposite Luxor). In 1899 Carter was appointed first chief inspector general of Monuments for Upper Egypt, an area that included ancient Thebes, where he supervised a number of excavations. In 1905 Carter resigned his position after an incident concerning Egyptian archaeology site guards and a group of drunken French tourists where he supported the Egyptians' rights to defend themselves.

In 1907 Carter met the wealthy amateur Egyptologist and Fifth Earl of Carnarvon George Herbert, when he became the sponsor of the excavations at Deir el-Bahri and asked Carter to supervise the work. Between 1915 and 1922 Carter undertook a series of excavations in the Valley of the Kings, ancient Egypt's royal burial ground, financed by Lord Carnarvon. Carter had been determined to find the tomb of a pharaoh named Tutankhamun since learning about a cache of funeral goods recovered in a 1907 excavation sponsored by American lawyer Theodore M. Davis. The funerary deposit had been discovered in the Valley of the Kings in an unfinished tomb known as KV54, and contained seal impressions with the name of a little-known pharaoh called Tutankhamun. Davis thought Tomb KV54 to be Tutankhamun's complete tomb, and left it at that, but Carter believed that the real tomb lay in the Valley of the Kings waiting to be discovered. However, by 1922, after seven years of searching, no trace of the tomb of the obscure pharaoh had been found and Carnarvon was ready to withdraw his funding from the excavations.

Howard Carter's excavation diaries state that the season's excavations in the Valley of the Kings began on November 1, 1922, around the entrance to the tomb of Ramses VI. Carter and his team soon discovered the remains of the ancient stone huts built by Necropolis workmen, parts of which they had found on a previous excavation. It took the team a few days to clear the huts and then, at 10 a.m. on November 4th, underneath the position of the first hut, Carter discovered a step that proved to be the beginning of a staircase, which had been cut into the bedrock about 13 feet below the entrance of Ramses VI's tomb. The team spent the rest of the day and most of the next day, November 5th, clearing the debris from the staircase, and then around sunset Carter discovered a doorway sealed with the Royal Necropolis seal, showing the jackal-headed god Anubis (symbolizing a king) over nine enemies. Carter confided in his usually sober excavation diary that he felt "on the verge of what looked like a magnificent discovery—an untouched tomb."[2] He then made his way out of the tomb and returned home, sending a cable to Lord Carnarvon in England that must have made the aristocrat's heart jump: "At last have made wonderful discovery in Valley a magnificent tomb with seals intact recovered same for your arrival congratulations."[3]

As news spread of the discovery of an unplundered tomb in the Valley of the Kings, Carter and his workmen continued clearing the area around Ramses VI's tomb, finding more stone worker's huts and making preparations for the opening of the tomb on Carnarvon's arrival. On November 20th, Lord Carnarvon and his daughter, Lady Evelyn Herbert, arrived in Cairo, and on the 25th they were at the entrance to the tomb in the Valley of the Kings when the first stone doorway was opened to reveal a descending passage completely blocked with stone and rubble. After the laborious clearing of this passageway, on the afternoon of the following day, November 26th, Carter discovered a second sealed doorway, almost the same as the first with similar seal impressions. Unable to restrain himself any further, Carter made a hole in the top of the doorway and, using a candle, looked inside. He describes in his excavation diary what he saw:

> It was sometime before one could see, the hot air escaping caused the candle to flicker, but as soon as one's eyes became accustomed to the glimmer of light the interior of the chamber gradually loomed before one, with its strange and wonderful medley of extraordinary and beautiful objects heaped upon

one another…. With the light of an electric torch as well as an additional candle we looked in. Our sensations and astonishment are difficult to describe as the better light revealed to us the marvellous collection of treasures: two strange ebony-black effigies of a King, gold sandalled, bearing staff and mace, loomed out from the cloak of darkness; gilded couches in strange forms, lion-headed, Hathor-headed, and beast infernal; exquisitely painted, inlaid, and ornamental caskets; flowers; alabaster vases…; strange black shrines with a gilded monster snake appearing from within;…finely carved chairs; a golden inlaid throne;…stools of all shapes and design, of both common and rare materials; and, lastly a confusion of overturned parts of chariots glinting with gold, peering from amongst which was a mannikin.[4]

The following day, Ibrahim Effendi, the local inspector of the Department of Antiquities at Luxor, arrived and, with the help of electric light, the tomb was fully explored for the first time in 3,000 years. The incredible material in the first chamber (the antechamber of the tomb) was in complete disorder, a sign of the ancient intruders mentioned previously. Carter and Carnarvon discovered a sealed doorway (broken open in antiquity) inside the room that led to another chamber (the annex of the tomb). Inside the annex, Carter states in his diary that he came upon a "mass of furniture. An utter confusion of beds, chairs, boxes, alabaster and faience vases, statuettes"; again there were obvious signs of ancient looting with "every sort of thing overturned and searched for valuables."[5] But although Carter knew he had found the tomb of Tutankhamun (later designated KV62), there was still no trace of the mummy. On Wednesday, November 29th, the tomb was officially opened and a special report despatched to *The Times* in London via a runner sent to Luxor. A few days later the tomb was closed up, and Carter left for Cairo to arrange for a steel gate to be made for the inner doorway of the tomb to protect against any attempts at looting the priceless artifacts inside. After the gate was fixed on December 22nd, the tomb was opened to European and Egyptian press, and a few days later the long and arduous task of recording, photographing, and removing the items from the two tomb chambers and cataloguing them began.

Carter's diary for March 20, 1923, notes that he left for Cairo due to the illness of Lord Carnarvon, who had contracted blood poisoning thought to have been caused by an infected mosquito bite on the cheek. The next day Carter describes Carnarvon as "very ill with an acute attack of erysipelas and blood poisoning"[6] and on the 26th writes that he had developed pneumonia. Carnarvon died early in the morning on April 5th in the Continental-Savoy Hotel in Cairo, less than two months after the official opening of the burial chamber of Tutankhamun, which has led to a wealth of speculation (which we will come to later).

In 1924 and 1925, during the fourth and fifth seasons of excavation, Carter uncovered and examined the actual burial chamber of Tutankhamun, with most of the work being done on the coffin and sarcophagus in October 1925. The burial chamber was the only decorated chamber in the tomb, which is unusual in Egyptian royal tombs, where it was common for most of the walls to be decorated with scenes from the Book of the Dead. This absence of decoration may be more evidence that Tutankhamun's tomb was originally intended for a private individual and had to be adapted for royalty. The tomb's burial chamber contained four gilded wooden shrines nestled one inside the other; the outer shrine measured 16.66 feet in length, 10.76 feet in width, and 9.02 feet in height, and took up almost the entire room. The innermost shrine contained a quartzite sarcophagus that itself contained two gilded wooden coffins and an incredible solid gold coffin, inside of which was Tutankhamun's mummy. The three coffins fitted inside each other rather like Russian matryoshka dolls.

On October 28th the mummy of the boy king was revealed, with his exquisitely made gold death mask, which has become for many people the emblem of ancient Egypt. Carter and his staff carried out a thorough, four-day examination of the mummy, carefully unwrapping the bandages and recording the artifacts that had been secreted inside. They began work on the treasury of Tutankhamun's tomb in October 1926, and by November 1930 the entire contents of the tomb—the antechamber, annex, burial chamber, and treasury—had been cleared out.

2.2. *Tutankhamun's gold funerary mask. Image copyright by Jon Bodsworth. Courtesy of Wikipedia.*

A huge treasure of more than 5,000 items was discovered in Tutankhamun's tomb. When they had been photographed and recorded, most items were shipped to Cairo, where they are now held in the Museum of Egyptian Antiquities. Roughly 700 artifacts were discovered in the antechamber, which seemed to contain the objects used by the pharaoh in his everyday life and had been deposited in this chamber to follow him into the afterlife. The astonishing array of artifacts included richly decorated dismantled wooden chariots; three gilded wooden couches in the form of a lion, a cow, and the goddess Ammut (who was part hippopotamus, part crocodile, and part lioness); a cedar chair with its legs carved like the paws of a lion and decorated with a winged sun-disc with gold-foil overlay; and Tutankhamun's throne, a beautifully crafted wooded chair overlaid with sheet gold and silver, and inlaid with motifs in faience and semiprecious stones. The main panel of this golden throne is beautifully decorated with a scene showing a seated Tutankhamun being anointed with scented oil by his queen, Ankhesenamun.

The annex was the smallest room in Tutankhamun's tomb and yielded 280 objects, including a superbly carved and painted alabaster boat, valuable oils, foods, wines, pottery, stools, baskets, and a number of gaming boards for the game of Senet. Almost the whole area of the burial chamber was taken up by the shrines, so it could not be filled with burial artifacts. Tutankhamun's mummy, however, contained more than 100 items, intended as magical protection for the king, including an impressive Horus pendant made of gold inlaid with semi-precious stones. King Tutankhamun's gold royal crown, with inlays of glass and semiprecious stones, was found on the head of his mummy, as was the greatest of all treasures from the tomb, the king's death mask, weighing about 24 pounds and made of gold inlaid with blue glass. The gold emblems on the forehead of the mask of a vulture and cobra symbolize the king's sovereignty over Upper and Lower Egypt.

2.3. *Tutankhamun's gold funerary mask in the Egyptian Museum. Image by Bjorn Christian Torrissen. Licensed under the Creative Commons Attribution-Share Alike 3.0 Unported license on Wikipedia.*

The treasury room, as its name suggests, was full of an incredible array of objects, including ceremonial model boats, a gilded wooden statuette of Tutankhamun on a skiff throwing a harpoon, an elaborately decorated wooden chest overlaid with carved and painted ivory, and a wooden figure of Anubis, the jackal-headed god of mummification, mounted on a gilded shrine with carrying poles. The Anubis shrine had been positioned at the entrance to guard the chamber. Also discovered in the treasury was the king's stunning gilded wood canopic shrine, with four figures of guardian goddesses (Selket, Isis, Nepthys, and Neith), also made of gilded wood, on its sides. Inside this shrine was Tutankhamun's canopic chest, which had been carved from a single block of semi-translucent calcite, and inside this were four finely carved alabaster canopic jars containing the organs of the king.

After the excavations of Tutankhamun's tomb came to an end in 1932, Howard Carter returned to London, retiring from archaeology and undertaking part-time work as an agent for museums and private collectors, while at the same time working on the publication of his findings from the Valley of the Kings. But on March 2, 1939, he died of lymphoma, a type of cancer, in Kensington, London, at the age of 64, before he was able to fully publish his discoveries. The relatively early deaths of Lord Carnarvon and Howard Carter, as well as of others connected with the excavation of Tutankhamun's tomb, have led to stories of some kind of pharaoh's curse. We should not be too surprised at this, as most great ancient treasures are prone to attract a curse or two, as this book shows. Shortly after the tomb was opened in 1923 a British novelist with an interest in the mystical, Marie Corelli (pseudonym of Mary Mackay), issued a dramatic warning that was published in the *New York World* in which she said that "the most dire punishment follows any rash intruder into a sealed tomb."[7] There were stories that an ancient Egyptian warning had been found inside the tomb and when Lord Carnarvon died six weeks after the tomb had been opened, Arthur Conan Doyle, the creator of Sherlock Holmes and by that time a convinced Spiritualist, suggested his death had been caused by "elementals" or "curses" concocted by ancient Egyptian priests to guard the tomb of King Tutankhamun. But no such curse had ever been found inside the tomb.

The idea of a "mummy's curse" that ensured the early death of those who entered the tomb was promoted by newspapers seeking to increase their sales no matter what the facts of the situation were. Access to the reports from Carter's excavations was also limited, leaving many newspapers without a direct source of information in the Valley of the Kings, a situation perfect for the invention of juicy stories relating to deadly ancient pathogens being released on the opening of the tomb and such like. However, a 2002 study by Dr. Mark Nelson from Monash University in Australia, the results of which were published in the *British Medical Journal,* found that the 25 Western members of Carter's team (his study did not include Egyptians due to the difference in life expectancy between Westerners and Egyptians) who entered the tomb lived to an average age of 70. Lord Carnarvon's early death was in large measure the result of an automobile accident in Germany in 1901, which crushed his jaw, and punctured his chest and lung. The accident left him with an extremely weak immune system, and his doctor advised him to seek a warmer climate — hence his trips to Egypt. Howard Carter, who one would assume would be most at risk from any pharaoh's curse, lived more than 17 years after discovering the tomb.

Throughout his time in Egypt, Lord Carnarvon built up a collection of Egyptian antiquities from excavations and purchase from Egyptian bazaars and private individuals. On his death this collection was divided up, with some pieces being donated to the British Museum and to Newbury Museum (in Berkshire in the south of England). The bulk, though, of the artifacts went to the United States, and some of them are now in the Metropolitan Museum of Art in New York. In 2009 an Egyptian Exhibition opened at Highclere Castle, the country seat of the Earl of Carnarvon, in Hampshire, in the south of England, perhaps best known for its role as the main setting for the hugely popular British television period drama *Downton Abbey.* The exhibition included reproductions of some of the items uncovered by Howard Carter in Tutankhamun's tomb, as well as a number of smaller items from royal tombs in the Valley of the Kings. The exhibition drew the wrath of Zahi Hawass, at the time the secretary general of Egypt's Supreme Council of Antiquities, who stated that the objects on display were taken from Egypt illegally and should be returned immediately.

Various treasures from Tutankhamun's tomb have been exhibited throughout the years in a number of different countries throughout the world. The *Tutankhamun Treasures* exhibit traveled to 18 cities in the United States and six in Canada between 1961 and 1967; the *Treasures of Tutankhamun* exhibition, which contained 50 objects from the tomb, opened on March 30, 1972, in the British Museum and is still the most popular exhibition in the Museum's history. From London the exhibit moved on to the USSR, West Germany, the United States, and Canada. More recently *Tutankhamun and the Golden Age of the Pharaohs*, which again featured 50 artifacts from Tutankhamun's tomb, as well as objects from other 18th-century royal burials, began in 2004 in Basel, Switzerland, and went to Bonn, Germany, then to various cities in the United States. From November 15, 2007, to August 31, 2008, the exhibition was at the O2 in London, and in 2011 it finished in the Melbourne Museum, Australia, where it broke all records for touring exhibitions in the country, attracting almost 800,000 visitors. Today Tutankhamun's mummy still lies in his tomb in the Valley of the Kings where Howard Carter discovered it 90 years ago. For a number of years the tomb was closed to the public while restoration work was undertaken, but in November 2012 the Egyptian government had the tomb reopened in an attempt to revive the flagging post-revolution tourist industry in the country.

# The Gold of Troy: Priam's Treasure

In 1873 wealthy German businessman and amateur archaeologist Heinrich Schliemann discovered a huge hoard of 3,000-year-old gold and other valuable artifacts at the supposed site of ancient Troy, in modern-day northwest Turkey. Known as Priam's Treasure, after the Homeric king of Troy, most of this incredible collection was later smuggled out of the country to Berlin, where it remained until 1945, when it disappeared from a bunker beneath the Berlin Zoo. Nothing more was heard of the hoard for decades, though it was suspected that the Red Army had stolen it from the bunker when they captured the city (though Russia always denied this). However, in 1993 Priam's Treasure was discovered at the Pushkin Museum in Moscow. In 1990 an agreement was reached between the Russian and the German governments to return the works of art stolen during WWII, but protracted negotiations between the two countries have not resolved the issue and the collection remains in Russia. Further complicating the matter, Turkey has also claimed ownership of the treasure, which it says was illegally removed from its territory by Schliemann. Perhaps more controversially in recent years are the allegations questioning the authenticity of Priam's Treasure, suggesting that the artifacts are in fact 19th-century forgeries, probably assembled by Schliemann himself.

Schliemann's sensational archaeological discoveries at the Bronze Age sites of Mycenae and Tiryns in Greece, and Troy in northwest Turkey, during the 1870s and 1880s made him a celebrated public figure. The revelation that the supposedly mythical Troy of Homer was a real city whose ruins Schliemann had discovered captured the public imagination in a way never equaled until Howard Carter found the tomb of 14th-century BC pharaoh Tutankhamun in the Valley of the Kings in 1922. The image of Schliemann's beautiful Greek wife, Sophia, wearing part of Priam's Treasure known as "the Jewels of Helen," made an indelible impression on the public's mind at the time and helped to bring the world of Homeric heroes and their long-suffering wives into the modern world.

3.1. Sophia Schliemann, wife of Heinrich Schliemann, wearing treasures discovered at Hisarlik. Courtesy of Wikipedia.

But behind all the pomp of the apparent discovery of Homer's Troy lies a rather different story, where questions remain over the most basic of Schliemann's assertions about the site of Troy, and his version of events of the discovery and subsequent fate of Priam's Treasure.

Born on January 6, 1822, in the town of Neubukow, Mecklenburg-Vorpommern, northern Germany, Heinrich Schliemann was the son of a Protestant minister. Heinrich's father read his son the captivating tales of classic literature from an early age, and Heinrich became particularly engrossed by Homer's poems, especially *The Iliad*. After the early death of his mother when he was 9, Heinrich was sent to live with an uncle and five years later was apprenticed to a small grocer, where he worked for five years before a back injury forced him to leave. Looking for more adventurous employment, in 1841, at the age of 19, Schliemann signed on as a cabin boy on a ship sailing for Colombia, but the vessel sank during a hurricane off the coast of Holland. The young man's luck was in, and along with the captain and one other crew member, he was washed ashore and eventually found his way to Amsterdam. There he obtained a job as a clerk and later, in 1844, as a correspondent and bookkeeper at Messrs. B. H. Schroder & Co., a large import and export firm. It was around this time that Schliemann discovered he had an amazing flair for languages, which eventually enabled him to learn, if accounts are to be believed, English, ancient and modern Greek. French, Dutch, Spanish, Portuguese, Swedish, Danish, Polish, Italian, Greek, Latin, Russian, Arabic, and Turkish.

In 1846 the firm sent him to St. Petersburg as their commercial agent. In Russia Schliemann flourished, soon founding his own company to sell commodities such as indigo, sugar, tea, coffee, and wine, while remaining employed by Schroder & Co. He also visited the United States where he apparently made a fortune in the Californian gold rush. Back in Russia in 1852, he married Ekaterina Petrovna Lyshin, with whom he had a son and two daughters. Schliemann's astute business sense, illustrated by becoming a military contractor during the Crimean War (1853–1856) and investing in American and Cuban railways and Brazilian bonds, brought him great wealth but not happiness. In 1863, at the age of 41, Schliemann gave up his business in order to devote his time and fortune to his interests, particularly his childhood love of Homer. In 1868 he traveled to Greece, trying to locate the sites visited by Ulysses in Homer's epic, from which emerged his book *Ithaka, der Peloponnes und Troja* (1869). He also divorced his Russian wife and, though his friend the Archbishop of Athens, met

17-year-old Sophia Engastromenos, whom he married in October 1869. But Schliemann's main obsession was to find the site of the ancient city of Troy, which by now he had concluded from his research was either at Hisarlik, a site near the Dardanelles in northwest Turkey, or at Bali Dagh, a hill overlooking the village of Bunarbashi, not far from Hisarlik.

Schliemann was far from being the first to believe that ancient Troy lay at Hisarlik. In 1822 Scottish journalist Charles Maclaren published *A Dissertation on the Topography of the Plain of Troy,* claiming that the fable Homeric city lay within the huge mound at Hisarlik. But the real pioneer in the hunt for Troy was English scholar and Consular agent for the United States at the Dardanelles Frank Calvert (1828–1908). The Calvert family had arrived in the Troad (modern-day Biga peninsula, in northwest Turkey) in 1829, and in 1847 Frank's brother Frederick bought a 2,000-acre farm at Akca Koy that included about half of Mount Hisarlik, the other half being owned by the Turkish government. Frank Calvert believed the mound contained an important archaeological site and began careful trial excavations there in 1863, carrying on until 1865, though crucially he never published his findings. Calvert's discoveries from the excavations and his topographical knowledge of the area soon convinced him that he had discovered the site of Troy, and he sent a request for financial assistance to the British Museum. The request, however, was rejected, perhaps because of the notoriety surrounding the family due to a shipping swindle involving his brother Frederick, who was imprisoned (probably wrongly) in 1868 for his part in the fraud. Constantly unable to find sponsorship for full excavations of the site, Calvert must have thought his luck had turned one day in the late summer of 1868 when Heinrich Schliemann arrived at Hisarlik, searching for the site of Troy, and with seemingly endless resources at his disposal.

Realizing that Schliemann could provide the financial backing he needed, Calvert convinced him that Hisarlik was indeed the site of Homer's Troy and gave the businessman a detailed description of his excavations there. Soon afterward Schliemann applied for a *firman* (permit or license) from the Turkish government to excavate the whole mound of Hisarlik. Schliemann believed that Troy would have been the first city built on the site, and therefore at the bottom of the great mound. Realizing the amount of work to be done and impatient to begin, Schliemann started his excavations in 1870, before the firman arrived. It soon became obvious that he and Calvert had decidedly different approaches to archaeological excavation—Calvert slow and methodical, Schliemann rushed and haphazard. The longed-for firman finally arrived in August 1871, and Schliemann began official excavations with 70 or 80 workmen on October 11th and dug until November 24th. One of the terms stated in the firman was that any treasure found must be divided with the government; another declared that all walls discovered must be left in place. As we shall see, Schliemann was to ignore both of these stipulations.

All Schliemann's excavation work was concentrated on the western part of the mound—that which belonged to the Turkish government rather than Calvert, and although he managed to reach a depth of 13 feet, destroying great blocks of stone wall and various levels of archaeological history in the process, he could identify nothing Homeric. But Schliemann was not a man to be so easily disheartened. During excavations on Calvert's part of Hisarlik in June 1872, Schliemann and Calvert discovered an architectural sculpture showing the sun god Helios riding the four horses of the sun, dating from the early Hellenistic period (c 300 BC–c 280 BC) and therefore much later than the time of Homer. Schliemann paid Calvert $200 for the sculpture, a fraction of its real worth, and later it and various other artifacts from the dig were smuggled out of the country and ended up decorating the garden of Schliemann's house in Athens.

Finally, in August 1872, Schliemann's team discovered the skeleton of a woman that showed signs of burning, accompanied by gold earrings, silver armbands, and a dress pin. The woman, Schliemann decided, must have died during the sack of Troy by the Greeks. This discovery gave Schliemann renewed hope for his third digging campaign, which began in February 1873, and in May of that year he uncovered a gate and a portion of the defensive walls of a settlement. Schliemann pronounced that this must be the famous Scaean Gate, the celebrated entrance-way to Priam's Troy and where, according to Homer, Paris had killed Achilles with a single arrow. Ever the self-publicist, Schliemann kept the public informed of his archaeological discoveries through his dispatches to the London *Times* and the *Daily Telegraph,* as well as a number of other newspapers; consequently he felt that the pressure was on him to back up his theories with hard evidence in the form of spectacular finds.

On or around May 31, 1873, the day before the season's digging finished, Schliemann and his workmen were excavating near the walls of what he believed was Priam's Troy. Suddenly they came upon a large copper vessel, and Schliemann's eager eye spotted a glint of gold inside it. In order that he could (according to his diary) "withdraw the treasure from the greed of my workmen, and to save it for archaeology,"[1] Schliemann called lunch break, during which time he cut the treasure out of the ground with a large knife and with the help of his wife, Sophia, who carried objects in her shawl, took the treasure off site. Schliemann then had the collection taken to Frederick Calvert's farm at Akca Koy, about 4 miles south of Hisarlik. The problem with this account of the famous discovery, as Schliemann later admitted, was that at the time it was made, Sophia was in Athens with her family, after the death of her father. In the following week Schliemann had the treasure packed up in chests and smuggled out of the country by ship to Greece, without a word to the Turkish authorities. All this was done without Schliemann having recorded details about the exact level and find spots of the valuable artifacts he had discovered, which of course led to doubts about whether the objects had all been found in the same part of the site or at the same level.

Nevertheless, in August 1873, when Schliemann published his discovery of "Priam's Treasure" at Troy it caused a sensation. The fabulous riches he had uncovered included an incredible collection of gold and silver diadems (two particularly striking gold diadems had attached gold pendants), bracelets, earrings, pendants, rings, plates, vases, goblets, knife blades, buttons, cups, and perfume jars, as well as ceremonial stone axes, copper lance heads, daggers, and axes. The treasure was huge; the gold rings and buttons alone accounted for 8,750 items. But what did this incredibly rich collection of objects represent? Was it a sacrifice to the gods at some particularly hazardous time in Troy's history? Or could this event have been Homer's Trojan War?

Unfortunately for him, Schliemann's publication of his incredible finds also attracted the unwanted attention of the Turkish authorities, who, understandably enraged that the objects had been smuggled out of their country, withdrew their permission for Schliemann to excavate and sued him for a share of the treasure. After much negotiation the Turks eventually won a $5,000 judgment. In the meantime Schliemann turned his attention to Greece and, in August 1876, began excavating at the Bronze Age site of Mycenae, in the northeastern Peloponnese, alongside the Greek Archaeological Society. Again following Homer, and also Pausanias, the second-century AD Roman traveler, Schliemann was looking for royal tombs, perhaps even that of Homeric Greek King Agamemnon himself. The German's luck proved not to have deserted him, and by November his excavation within the city walls had revealed Shaft Graves (Tombs) containing the skeletons of several Mycenaean chieftains, five of whom were wearing gold face masks, and a host of other rich burial goods. Eventually these spectacular finds were shown to be at least 300 years earlier than the supposed date of the Trojan War (believed by scholars to have been some time in the 12th century BC), and the authenticity of one of the finds, known as the Mask of Agamemnon, has been called into question.

Encouraged by his findings at Mycenae, Schliemann now wanted to go back to excavate at Troy. In order to facilitate this he paid the Turkish government back $25,000 for the previous finds he had removed from the country and was granted a firman to excavate beginning in 1878. This time, however, Schliemann's excavations would be closely monitored by the authorities.

In August of the same year, some of the objects Schliemann had excavated at Hisarlik were sent to London to be exhibited at the South Kensington Museum (now the Victoria and Albert Museum), the last time the treasure would be seen in public for more than a 100 years.

Schliemann excavated at Hisarlik in three separate seasons, from 1878 to 1879, from 1882 to 1883, and finally from 1888 to 1890. In 1881, accompanied by Sophia, he traveled to Berlin, where he ceremoniously handed over Priam's Treasure to the German people. The exquisite collection was afterward divided between two adjacent Berlin museums, the Museum of Applied Arts and Design (inside the Martin Gropius building) and the Ethnographical Museum (later renamed the Museum of Early and Pre-History), where a room was dedicated to Schliemann's finds. Various other items from Schliemann's later digs at Hisarlik were also subsequently donated to Berlin museums.

The final series of excavations at Hisarlik, from 1888 to 1890, were undertaken alongside German architect and archaeologist Wilhelm Dörpfeld (1853–1940), a pioneer of the method of dating archaeological sites based on the strata in which objects are found. Dörpfeld was to teach Schliemann much about careful archaeological excavation, and it was he who continued excavations at Hisarlik after Schliemann died in Naples in December 1890, a few days after visiting Pompeii. Schliemann's funeral in Athens was an elaborate affair attended by the king of Greece, various government ministers, and the cream of Athenian society. He was buried in a luxurious mausoleum at the First Cemetery in Athens, practically a temple to his achievements, decorated with scenes from the *Iliad* and the *Odyssey,* and a portrait of him excavating at Troy holding a copy of Homer. Frank Calvert, meanwhile, died at his farm on August 12, 1908, and was buried in the small family cemetery at Çanakkale in the Dardanelles.

Along with later excavators of Troy Carl Blegen and Dr. Manfred Osman Korfmann, Dörpfeld's work revealed that there were at least nine cities built one on top of each other at the site. Furthermore, the city Schliemann had believed was Homer's Troy (known as Troy II) was later revealed to have been much too old, dating from around 2600 BC to 2250 BC. The general consensus among archaeologists now is that Troy VIIa (c mid-13th century BC–1190 BC) is the most likely candidate for Homer's Troy. Despite these archaeological facts, Priam's Treasure and the archaeological remains Schliemann discovered at Hisarlik are still associated with Homer's Troy in the public mind.

But what of the treasure itself?

In 1902 German scholar Hubert Schmidt cataloged the pieces from Schliemann's excavations at Hisarlik, at that time numbering 9,704 pieces, and divided them into no less than 19 separate "treasure" hoards, identified by the letters A through S. Schmidt designated "Priam's Treasure" itself (defined as the objects discovered at the end of May 1873) as "Treasure A."

For a long time it was believed that Priam's Treasure had been destroyed during the Battle of Berlin, fought between April and May 1945, and the last major offensive of WWII. During the battle the Red Army defeated the German forces, and the fall of the city would lead to the surrender of the Germans and the end of WWII. But as it turned out, Schliemann's luck had continued even long after his death. Before the beginning of WWII, Hitler had ordered that all works of art held in Berlin should be classified into three categories: Class 1 (Irreplaceable; usually gold and precious metal/stones objects), Class 2 (Very Valuable; usually silver objects), or Class 3 (Other). The objects in Schliemann's Treasure fell into all three categories and were thus separated into three Class 1 crates (the most valuable gold objects were packed in a crate numbered MVF 1), 30 Class 2 crates, and a number of Class 3 crates. In August 1939, just a week before the German invasion of Poland, the museum in the Gropius Building was closed and the crates were moved to the basement for safekeeping. Allied bombs began dropping on the city in August 1940, and in January 1941 the crates were moved again, some of them to the Prussian Maritime Commercial bank and others to the cellar of the New Mint, part of the Reichsbank building. In September and November, the crates were transferred to a bunker beneath the

Zoo flak tower, a gigantic anti-aircraft defense tower in the Tiergarten district, next to the Berlin Zoological Garden.

However, during the chaos of the Battle of Berlin in April–May 1945, the crates containing Priam's Treasure and other valuables were located by members of the Red Army, and left Berlin by air on June 30th, heading for Russia. Crate MVF 1 containing the gold objects was flown to Moscow; the silver objects were sent to St. Petersburg (then called Leningrad). That was the last anyone heard of Priam's Treasure. During the succeeding Cold War years Russia repeatedly denied any knowledge of what had happened to the collection, and all hope seemed lost that Schliemann and Calvert's discoveries from Troy would ever be seen again.

Then, in August 1993, the Russian government made a startling announcement. It reported from Moscow that it had been storing Priam's Treasure in the basement of the Pushkin Museum since the end of the war, and that it was about to put the objects on display. It took a while, but on April 6, 1996, "The Treasures of Troy from the Collection of Heinrich Schliemann" was exhibited at the Pushkin Museum of Fine Arts in Moscow. But was this all of Schliemann's treasure? There were 260 individually cataloged items in the exhibit, but some items are obviously made up of many smaller pieces, such as necklaces, some of which contain as many as 200 individual beads. Consequently scholars have estimated that there are around 12,000 single pieces (representing 13 of the original 19 treasures) in the collection at the Pushkin Museum. Included in the collection is of course Treasure A (Priam's Treasure), which once consisted of 183 objects, 101 of which are held in the Pushkin Museum. The State Hermitage Museum in St. Petersburg has 414 inventoried bronze items from Troy, including spearheads, knives, chisels, pins, toggle-pins, needles, sickles, hammer-axes, and flat axes, and also 55 clay pots. Other items from the caches of artifacts from Troy are believed to be scattered among various museums and private collectors around the world.

The 1996 exhibit had another, perhaps unexpected, effect. Once it became known that Priam's Treasure had been in Russia all along, the German government made a claim on the items. The Russian government, however, replied as it has done to all German claims on what it calls "trophy art" (looted German art): that such art treasures taken at the end of WWII are appropriate compensation for damage done to its country during the conflict (see the chapter on the Amber Room for more on this issue). Since then, years of negotiations between Germany and Russia for the return of Priam's Treasure (and many other stolen works of art) to Berlin have taken place without a mutually acceptable solution having been reached. Turkey, too, has made claims on Schliemann's treasure, naturally enough (as Troy is in Turkey). Another claim, at least on part of the treasure, came not from a country but from a family.

In 1996 it was announced that British and American heirs of Frank Calvert were filing a claim for a part of Schliemann's treasure discovered on Calvert's land. Working from Schliemann's notebooks British archaeologist and member of Manfred Korfmann's excavation team at Troy, Dr. Donald F. Easton, has discovered that Treasure L from Hisarlik, a particularly rich hoard of ceremonial axes and various rock crystal objects discovered in 1890, was located in Calvert's part of the mound. Although Calvert's heirs would appear to have had a legitimate claim, the treasure still remains at the Pushkin Museum. Perhaps the best suggestion was made by Dr. Easton in 1995 in the journal *Antiquity* that there should be "an internationally-sponsored museum" erected at the site of Troy "where Trojan material from collections in all countries can be gathered on permanent loan."[2]

Throughout the years another point of contention regarding Priam's Treasure has been its genuineness. For years after Schliemann's discoveries were made public there were rumors that he had in fact hired a jeweler to manufacture "ancient" jewelry that he then distributed throughout the site. However, there has never been any evidence produced to support this theory. Indeed a number of academics, including Dr. Manfred Korfman and Dr. Donald Easton, closely examined a number of items from Priam's Treasure in Moscow in 1994 and found them to be genuine.

But perhaps the most controversial claims surrounding the authenticity of Schliemann's discoveries at Troy are those made by Dr. David A. Traill, a classics professor at the University of California. The most pointed of Traill's allegations (summed up in his 1997 book, *Schliemann of Troy: Treasure and Deceit*), is that Schliemann's own accounts of his discovery of Priam's Treasure (Treasure A) outside the city gates of Troy are not to be trusted (Traill calls him a "pathological liar"[3]) and it is more likely that the cache was in fact a collection of artifacts discovered at several places throughout the site on separate excavations between 1871 and 1873. Traill even goes as far as to suggest that Schliemann's finds were "augmented by purchases"[4] probably from local villagers or from dealers in Athens or Constantinople.

However, a number of archaeologists, including Donald F. Easton, have come to Schliemann's defense, saying that, though it is essential to be careful and critically minded when assessing Schliemann's work, his mistakes were more the result of eagerness and haste rather than outright deceit. Most archaeologists concur with Traill on one point, however: that there are grounds for believing that Schliemann's account of discovering Priam's Treasure in one place in July 1873 is not true, and that this hoard is probably an assemblage of artifacts from various parts of the site rather than a single collection. Although this is indeed a worrying fact, it should not detract from the importance of Schliemann's achievements at Troy and their lasting significance. Schliemann stated in his diaries, "If my memoirs...contain contradictions, I hope that these may be pardoned when it is considered that I have revealed a new world of archaeology."[5] No one can argue that with his excavations at Troy and his discoveries of thousands of fascinating artifacts, including Priam's Treasure, Schliemann did indeed reveal "a new world of archaeology."

# The Lydian Hoard (The Karun Treasure)

The Lydian Hoard is a priceless collection of 363 gold and silver artifacts dating to the sixth century BC and originating from tombs in ancient Lydia (modern western Turkey). Most of the collection was looted from the grave of a Lydian princess in the 1960s and sold on to a local antiquities dealer before finding its way to the Metropolitan Museum of Art in New York City by 1970. In 1986 a formal demand for return of the treasure was made by Turkey, but the request was rejected. In 1987 Turkey entered into what were to become drawn-out legal proceedings against the Met for the return of the Lydian Treasure, the case eventually being settled out of court in 1993. With whispers of a fatal curse being connected to the treasure, one or two people were not surprised when news broke in 2006 that one of the central pieces from the treasure on display in Uşak Museum in Turkey was, in fact, a fake, the original having been stolen about a year earlier. The former director of the Museum was the prime suspect in the case.

The Lydian Treasure is also known as the Karun Treasure after an extremely wealthy man in the *Koran,* and is sometimes also given the title the Treasures of Croesus, after the Lydian King Croesus. Croesus was ruler of Lydia from 560 BC to 547 BC and was renowned for his prodigious wealth (hence the expression "as rich as Croesus"). However, although the artifacts from the Lydian Hoard are contemporary with the reign of Croesus, there is no evidence that they are directly associated with him.

The part of Turkey that constituted ancient Lydia was both fertile and resource-rich; consequently settlement and civilization in the area dates at least as far back as the Chalcolithic Period (5500 BC–3200 BC). Lydia emerged as a Neo-Hittite kingdom following the collapse of the Hittite Empire in the 12th century BC, which had included at its height central Turkey, northwestern Syria, and Upper Mesopotamia (north eastern Syria and northern Iraq). At its greatest extent, the kingdom of ancient Lydia covered all of western Anatolia. Central Lydia, where the treasure originated, was the heartland of the Iron Age (sixth century BC) kingdom, which had its capital at Sardis (modern Sart in Manisa Province). Lydia lay at a cross-road of eastern and western cultures, and its rich culture shows traces of both Near Eastern and Greek influences. Indeed the Lydians were well known to the Greeks, and a number of their kings, including Alyattes and Croesus, sent rich offerings to the renowned oracle at Delphi. According to Greek historian Herodotus (c484 BC–425 BC) the Lydians were the first people to introduce gold and silver coins. Modern archaeology has proven Herodotus partly right, as the earliest known coins are indeed found mainly in parts of Lydia, although they are made from a naturally occurring mixture of gold and silver called electrum.

The heyday of the Lydian kingdom lasted from the seventh to the fourth centuries BC. The earliest ruler of the kingdom we know of is King Gyges, founder of the Mermnad dynasty, who reigned either from 716 BC to 678 BC or from c680 BC–644 BC. Gyges is known to have established trade networks and political alliances with other states, and embarked on various military campaigns to conquer lands in the west of Lydia, thus increasing the power and wealth of the Lydian kingdom. One of the most important sources of Lydia's wealth at this time was the gold extracted from deposits washed down by the Pactolus River, the river on which the Lydian capital of Sardis lay. The Lydians used this gold dust in the manufacture of some of the world's first coins.

Alyattes, king of Lydia from c610 BC until his death in 560 BC, is considered to be the founder of the Lydian empire, mainly due to the success of his military campaigns. He attacked the Greek city of Miletus, in western Anatolia, around 20 miles south of the present city of Söke, Tur; expelled the nomadic Cimmerians, who had previously attacked Sardis and killed the Lydian King Gyges; and fought a five-year campaign against King Cyaxares of the Medes (an ancient Iranian people). According to Herodotus, the war against the Medes was interrupted by a solar eclipse during a battle at the River Halys (now known as The Kızılırmak) on May 28, 585 BC. This momentous event apparently brought hostilities to an end, and a treaty was drawn up where a border between the great two powers was established at the River Halys.

During the reign of Alyattes's eldest son, King Croesus (the last king of the Mermnad dynasty), Lydia subjugated the Greek cities of mainland Ionia (on the west coast of Anatolia), including Ephesus and Smyrna. Allying himself with Egyptian pharaoh Amasis (who ruled 570 BC–526 BC), the Greek city state of Sparta, and Nabonidus of Babylonia, Croesus also decided to attack the emerging Persian Empire, which under Cyrus the Great had been threatening Lydia's eastern frontier. Before embarking on this campaign, Croesus consulted the oracle at Delphi, which gave the famously ambiguous response that if he marched against Persia he would destroy a great Empire. Encouraged by this reply, in 547 BC Croesus crossed the Halys and attacked, but the result of the battle was indecisive, and the Lydian king returned home and partly disbanded his army. However, he had severely underestimated the perseverance of Cyrus and his army. The Persian forces pursued the Lydians all the way to Sardis, where the two armies fought a battle on the plain north of the city (the Battle of Thymbra) in which the Lydians were easily defeated.

Croesus was either captured or killed during the fighting and Lydia became a satrapy (province) of the Achaemenid (first Persian) Empire. A certain Tabalus (546 BC–545 BC) was appointed by Persian ruler Cyrus the Great to be the first governor of the area.

4.1. *Jug from the Lydian Treasure. Image by Mr. Arif Solak. Licensed under the Creaitive Commons Attribution-Share Alike 3.0 Unported license on Wikipedia.*

In terms of archaeology, there is not a great deal remaining from the ancient kingdom of Lydia. One form of architecture that does remain is the monumental tumulus (burial mound), which the Lydians constructed over the tombs built to house the remains of their royalty. These mounds were constructed of earth and stones sometimes covering a stone-built grave chamber beneath. Lydian earthen mounds can be anything from just over 32 feet high to more than 130 feet high, but the colossal tomb of Alyattes, on the southern shore of the ancient Gygaean Lake (Lake Marmara), 6 miles to the northwest of Sardis, is 201.64 feet in height with a diameter of 1,165.06 feet, making it as high as many Egyptian pyramids. This colossal tomb, which Herodotus described as "the greatest work of human hands in the world, apart from the Egyptian and Babylonian,"[1] lies within the Lydian royal cemetery known as Bin Tepe ("thousand mounds"), where a total of 116 tumuli were recorded by Boston University's central Lydia Archaeological Survey in 2005. The Tomb of Alyattes was partially excavated in 1854 by Ludwig Peter Spiegelthal, the

Prussian consul in Smyrna, who discovered that the tomb, which had been constructed of highly polished blocks of marble, had already been plundered, and the sarcophagus and its contents removed.

The Lydian Hoard originated from at least three Iron Age burial mounds (Toptepe, İkiztepe, and Aktepe) located near the village of Güre, in the Uşak region of western Turkey, and from at least one other (the Harta-Abidintepe tumulus) located farther west in Kırkag˘aç-Manisa. Between 1965 and 1968, these tombs were looted by local villagers, who often went to great lengths to secure their plunder. After many nights unsuccessfully attempting to dig through the thick marble chamber door of the İkiztepe Tomb, a group of villagers from Güre dynamited the roof in order to get at the riches within. Once inside the tomb, the men discovered the wealthy burial of a Lydian princess and proceeded to plunder the collection of 2,600-year-old artifacts that had been placed alongside the ancient noblewoman, practically destroying the tomb and its mound in their frantic search for treasure. There is a particularly interesting example of the folklore surrounding treasures and treasure hunting in some of the reports of the thefts from the İkiztepe Tomb, which state that the looters entered the chamber at 6 a.m., on the 6th of June, 1966.

Further looting of local tumuli by the same villagers over the next couple of years added to their considerable haul from the royal İkiztepe Tomb. The treasures they had stolen now comprised gold jewelry, including a magnificent gold and glass pendant/brooch depicting a hippocamp with wings (in Phoenician and Greek mythology, the hippocamp is a sea-horse), exquisite gold and silver vessels, including a silver oinochoe (wine jug) with a handle in the shape of a human figure, and a silver alabastron (a vessel for holding oil or perfume) decorated with battle scenes, a pair of marble sphinxes, ivory and wood objects, and pieces of wall paintings. What the villagers now wanted to do with this treasure was to move it on before they were caught.

Between 1965 and 1968 the looters sold most of the artifacts to Ali Bayirlar, an antiquities dealer from Izmir, who quickly sold them on to a dealer in Europe, believed to be George Zacos in Switzerland. Zacos, in turn, sold the pieces to New York art dealer, John Klejman, from whom the Metropolitan Museum of Art acquired 200 pieces of the hoard (in three separate batches) by 1970 for $1.5 million. Some items from the hoard had been recovered from the looters by Turkish police before they could be sold on, after they had argued among themselves as to how the money from the treasures should be divided and one had informed the police. As in many cases of buried and recovered treasure, a good curse does not go amiss, and the Lydian Hoard does not disappoint, with tales of suicides, accidental deaths, insanity, and financial disasters apparently affecting all those involved in the initial looting of the Lydian tombs.

Despite rumors circulating of the Met's shady acquisition nothing more was heard of the Lydian Hoard for more than a decade. Indeed the treasure had been languishing in the Museum's storerooms for around 14 years before it was decided that some of the more exquisite pieces should be put on permanent display. However, rather than indicate the true origin of the objects, the Met simply labeled its 1984 exhibit of the collection "East Greek Treasure" and described the items as "fine vessels made of ceramic, stone, and precious metals (silver, gold, and bronze), exquisite jewelry, a range of sculpture and wall paintings, and ancient implements."[2] That the Met knew about the un-provenanced nature of the treasure is shown by the discovery of a number of documents, including minutes of the meeting of the acquisition committee of the Board of Trustees at which the acquisition of the Lydian Hoard was approved.

In 1984 Özgen Acar, a Turkish journalist who had been on the trail of the Lydian Treasure for a number of years, happened to be visiting the Met when he came upon the display of the 50 pieces that constituted the East Greek Treasure. Acar immediately noticed the resemblance between the objects on display and the description he had of the Lydian Hoard, and went straight to the Turkish Ministry of Culture with the shocking news. An investigation was launched, during which photographs from the Turkish police of items seized from the original looters in the 1960s were compared with the pieces at the Met. From this evidence it was obvious that the East Greek Treasures on display at the Museum were part of the Lydian Hoard. In July 1986, Turkey made a formal request to the Met for the return of the Treasure, sending its consul general over to the United States for a meeting with museum officials. The request, based on Turkey's contention that the objects in the hoard had been illegally excavated and taken out of the country, was, however, rejected.

In May 1987 Turkey filed a lawsuit in federal court against the Metropolitan Museum of Art, but the Met filed a motion to dismiss the claim on the basis that the three-year limitation period in the statute of limitations had expired. In 1990 this motion was denied. Further legal battles followed during which Turkey produced evidence for the illicit nature of the treasure, which included statements from the looters themselves and from museum officials at the Met. Due mainly to the weight of this evidence against them, in 1993 the Met agreed to settle out of court and the objects from the Lydian Hoard were returned to Turkey. The treasure first traveled to Istanbul, Ankara, and other Turkish cities before finally arriving in the one-room Uşak Museum in 1995, where it was to be exhibited alongside the other artifacts from the looted tombs recovered by the Turkish police in the 1960s.

The retrieval of the Lydian Hoard was a landmark achievement not only for Turkey but for all countries whose history and culture had been damaged by the actions of looters, unscrupulous museums, and the shady dealings of the illegal antiquities trade. The irony of the case, as noted by Özgen Acar, is that the Met had paid $1.5 million for the Lydian Hoard in the late 1960s, but had ended up spending at least twice that amount on legal expenses. However, this was not to be the end of the controversy surrounding the infamous treasure.

In April 2006 the "Treasures of Croesus" hit the headline again when major Turkish daily newspaper *Milliyet* published the sensational news that one of the main pieces from the collection, the golden hippocamp brooch, which was on prominent display in the Uşak Museum along with the rest of the collection, was in fact a fake. According to reports Kayhan Kavas, the governor of Uşak, had received an anonymous letter maintaining that the hippocamp brooch had been stolen, probably between March and August 2005, and replaced with a forgery. Worse news was to follow a few weeks later when it was announced that the director of the museum, Kazim Akbiyikoglu, was suspected of the theft. An official inquiry discovered that a coin and perhaps other pieces from the hoard had also gone missing. Akbiyikoglu protested his innocence, claiming that as far back as 1996, when the collection arrived at Uşak Museum from Ankara, he had realized that one piece was missing, although he had not noticed that the hippocamp brooch had been replaced by a counterfeit until March 2006. He also suggested that the brooch may have been switched with a fake during the time it was in the United States. However, Omer Erbil, the journalist who wrote the original piece on the theft in *Milliyet,* was quoted as saying that Akbiyikoglu was also being prosecuted for other crimes, including complicity to smuggle artifacts and gambling on museum premises. Erbil further added that Akbiyikoglu had "obstructed past attempts to count and inspect the Croesus treasures."[3]

In July 2006, 10 people, including Akbiyikoglu, were charged with "embezzlement and artifact smuggling in a case involving the theft of a piece of the famed Lydian Hoard at the Uşak Museum," according to the *Turkish Daily News.*[4] But it was not until January 2009 that a court in Uşak sentenced Kazim Akbiyiklioglu to 12 years and 11 months in prison for theft and embezzlement, and the nine other defendants received lesser prison terms. In November 2012, it was reported by the English-language Turkish newspaper the *Hurriyet Daily News* that the hippocamp brooch had been recovered in Germany.[5] The brooch, worth millions of dollars, is set to be returned home to Turkey, where it will receive pride of place in a new national museum, set to open in December 2013. Perhaps the curse of the Lydian Hoard is finally wearing off.

The case of the Lydian Hoard is one of the thousands of incidents of the looting of ancient sites from around the world, but the problem is particularly bad in western Turkey. Dr. Christopher H. Roosevelt, one of the directors of Boston University's Central Lydia Archaeological Survey, has written that during his 2001 survey, he discovered that of the 397 ancient tumuli he visited, 357 had been at least partially looted, with 72 of them having been completely destroyed. In Roosevelt's 2005 survey of the Bin Tepe cemetery, he found that a staggering 96 percent of the tumuli had been looted, with 18 destroyed. In 2008 Roosevelt's team revisited 18 of the tumuli in Bin Tepe, to discover that eight showed signs of recent looting, one within six weeks or so of their arrival. Perhaps the low point was reached during the 2007 survey, when the Boston University team found that the tomb-chamber opening of one tumulus had been cleared and was being used as a toilet.[6]

One important question about the looting of these ancient tombs is: Where are the stolen items going? There is obviously a huge demand for looted ancient Lydian artifacts on the international antiquities market, so it is inconceivable that the contents of hundreds of Lydian tombs have remained in Turkey. But beyond the fact that most if not all the valuable artifacts from Lydian tumuli leave Turkey via the city of Izmir and pass through the hands of dealers in Europe and the United States, we know little else. Unfortunately what we are left with is the sad fact that, due to the vast amount of looting taking place in western Turkey, archaeologists like Dr. Roosevelt are never allowed the opportunity to investigate untouched tumuli, and so gain important insights into the culture of the ancient Lydians and the archaeological landscape of western Turkey.

## The Treasure of Benghazi: Heist of the Century?

*D*uring the chaos of the civil war in Libya in 2011, there was a major robbery from a bank in the city of Benghazi. In what newspapers described as one of the biggest heists in archaeological history, thieves broke into the bank vault and made off with thousands of ancient coins, jewelry, and statuettes originally from the site of Cyrene in north east Libya. The so-called Treasure of Benghazi was never seen again, though there were reports of some items from the hoard turning up in the Benghazi gold market and in neighboring Egypt. However, there have been serious questions asked about the theft. For example, why, if the robbery took place in May 2011, did bank officials not report it until October 2011, and how, because the presence of the treasure in the bank vault was a closely guarded secret, did the thieves know it was there? The robbery also brings into focus the wider issue of the scale of looting in Libya during the conflict of 2011, with some archaeologists stating that the country's antiquities were safe despite the chaos, while other sources claimed that Libya's museums were being looted and ancient sites destroyed in NATO bombing raids.

The site of ancient Cyrene is located in modern Shahhat, a town in the District of Jebal al Akhdar ("Green Mountain") in northeastern Libya. The name Cyrene is derived from the ancient Greek *Kyre,* a spring on the site that the Greeks consecrated to the god Apollo. According to ancient Greek historian Herodotus (fifth century BC) Cyrene was founded in 631 BC by Greek emigrants from the island of Thera (modern Santorini), an island in the southern Aegean Sea, who, racked by famine, were advised by the Oracle at Delphi to send a colony to Libya. Located in a fertile valley, Cyrene soon flourished and developed into a major commercial and cultural center, eventually giving its name to the whole region: Cyrenaica. The success of Cyrene led to the establishment of four other Greek colonies in the region: Apollonia (the port of Cyrene, located in modern Susa), Barce (also known as Ptolemais, located near modern Al Marj), Tocra (originally Taucheira — on the coast to the northwest of Barce), and Euesperides, the westernmost of the colonies in Cyrenaica, situated on the outskirts of modern Benghazi. These five Greek colonies were collectively known as the Pentapolis.

*5.1. Archaeological site of Cyrene. Courtesy of Wikipedia.*

Cyrenaica was ruled as a republic from the mid-fifth century BC and was at the height of prosperity in the fifth and fourth centuries BC. The city's economy was based on the export of grain and the medicinal plant silphium. Silphium was exploited in a number of ways; perfume was extracted from its flowers, its stalk was used as food, and medicine was obtained from its juice and roots. As early as the seventh century BC Greek and Egyptian women were using the plant as a contraceptive. Indeed, silphium became so important for Cyrene's economy and way of life that it was depicted on the city's coinage for many years, though over-harvesting finally exhausted all supplies during the Roman period and the plant has long been extinct.

In 331 BC Cyrene was conquered by Alexander the Great, and after his death in 323 BC came under the control of the Greek general Ptolemy I and his dynasty. Cyrene became established as a Roman province in 74 BC, and enjoyed a lasting period of peace until the large scale destruction and massacres of the Jewish Revolt of AD 115. The city nevertheless recovered during the reign of Hadrian (Roman Emperor from AD 117 to AD 138) and entered a new age of prosperity that lasted throughout the second century AD. However, in AD 365 a huge earthquake and tidal wave hit the area and Cyrene began to decline, a process exacerbated by the growing aridity of the region and increasing attacks by nomadic tribes.

Despite the ravages of time, natural disaster, and warfare, the extant remains of ancient Cyrene are still some the largest and most impressive in the Mediterranean. Designated a World Heritage Site by United Nations Educational, Scientific and Cultural Organization (UNESCO) in 1982, the archaeological site of Cyrene includes the magnificent Sanctuary of Apollo, begun in the seventh century BC and containing temples to Apollo, Artemis, and the Egyptian goddess Isis, as well as an impressive fifth-century theater (later converted into an amphitheater by the Romans) and the second century AD Trajan Baths. The site also includes the huge Temple of Zeus, began in the fifth century BC but restored by the Romans, the late-seventh-century BC Sanctuary of Demeter and Persephone, various treasuries, an agora, and a large necropolis.

It is unclear just exactly when the Benghazi Treasure was excavated, though it is known that the hoard is a collection of various finds made by Italian archaeologists at sites in Libya, including Cyrene, while they occupied the country (from 1912 until 1942). Archaeological investigations at Cyrene go back a long way, and there were some attempts at excavation at the site by British teams in the mid-19th century. However, it was not until the early 20th century that any serious work was done. The Archaeological Institute of America excavated at Cyrene in 1910–1911 under the direction of Richard Norton, but on the morning of March 11, 1911, the expedition's epigrapher, Herbert Fletcher DeCou, was shot and killed by Arabs, and the excavations came to a close soon afterward.

Italian excavations at Cyrene began in late 1913 and carried on until 1942. Many items from the Benghazi treasure were apparently discovered by Italian archaeologists between 1917 and 1922 at the Temple of Artemis. Between 1928 and 1930 Luigi Pernier and Carlo Anti conducted excavations at the temple of Artemis as part of the Italian Archaeological Mission and uncovered a rich votive deposit that included seventh- and sixth-century BC pottery, terracotta figurines, and a number of objects of gold, silver, bronze, glass, amber, bone, and ivory. Pernier is famous for his discovery of the Phaistos Disc, a supposedly 14th-century BC inscribed clay disc, which he discovered in 1908 at the Minoan palace-site of Phaistos (second millennium BC) on Crete, though doubts persist as to the object's authenticity. However, the items excavated from the Temple of Artemis by the Italians are only a part — though a major part — of what is known as the Treasure of Benghazi. Other items from the treasure were excavated by Italian archaeologists in 1937 from the Late Hellenistic (c160 BC–30 BC) Roman Villa of the Columns at the ancient port of Ptolemais (formerly Barce), about halfway between Benghazi and

Susa. A third element of the treasure is a hoard of 2,000 coins known as the Meliu Collection, though little seems to be known about their origin.

Although there is no official list of what exactly the Benghazi Treasure comprised, it is believed that there were between 7,700 and as many as 10,000 objects, including 364 gold coins, 2,433 silver coins, and 4,484 bronze coins, of Greek, Roman, Byzantine, and early Islamic origin. There were also 306 pieces of ancient jewelry (including necklaces, bracelets, anklets, rings, gold earrings, gold armbands, and precious stones) and 43 other ancient objects including a gold foil plaque depicting a battle scene; various figurines of bronze, glass, ivory, and terracotta; Egyptian faïence scarabs; pottery; and a limestone head.

In 1942, when Allied forces invaded Libya, the Benghazi Treasure (or at least most of it; we do not have an inventory for this period) was packed up into two padlocked military chests and shipped to Italy, where it was displayed in the *Museo Coloniale* (Colonial Museum) of the Ministry of Italian Africa in Rome. In 1944 the chests were moved to the city of Cremona on the left bank of the Po River in northern Italy, and then to Val Brenta, in the Dolomites, in the northeast of the country. In 1961 the chests containing the treasure were finally returned to an independent Libya, when an inventory was apparently taken, though the objects were for some reason not photographed. Crucially, however, we do not know if the contents of the chests at this time included everything that the Italians had taken out of Libya in 1942. After the chests were returned to Libya, they were moved into two safes in the vaults of the National Commercial Bank in Omar al-Mukhtar Street, in the center of Benghazi. Unfortunately, during the Gaddafi regime scholars were forbidden from studying or documenting the collection, apart from the Islamic coins; consequently the contents of the chests were last checked as long ago as 1974. We know that in 1980 another collection of coins and artifacts from Benghazi was placed into the two safes, but apart from that the treasure remained in the vault largely forgotten about.

Toward the end of October 2011, at a conference in Paris held by UNESCO, details of an extraordinary robbery in Benghazi were revealed. Apparently, in the weeks following the taking of the city by rebel forces in February 2011, robbers broke into the National Bank, probably from a neighboring building, and drilled directly through a ceiling comprising more than 2 feet of steel-reinforced concrete and entered the vault. Then, probably using a circular saw, they sawed through the hinges of one safe and through the back of another to get at the wooden chests containing the treasure. The robbers then tore open the chests and took the most valuable of the ancient objects from inside. Items of lesser value in the vault were left untouched. On June 2nd, Fadel Ali Mohammed, chairman of the archaeology department of Libya's newly created National Transitional Council in Benghazi, wrote to the attorney general about the theft, which had in fact occurred on May 24th, and informed UNESCO in July. But why had it taken five months for details of the robbery to be announced to the public?

Hafed Walada, a Libyan archaeologist and a research fellow at King's College London, has said that that the robbery may have been an inside job carried out by robbers who knew exactly what they were looking for. Another archaeologist, Dr. Ahmed Buzaian, a professor of archaeology at Benghazi University, has also voiced his belief that the people who broke into the vault knew what was kept there and how valuable it was. The robbery certainly seems to have been well planned, and the thieves must have had advanced knowledge about the contents of the vaults, which points to there being some help from the inside—hence the delay in announcing the robbery. However, extensive questioning of bank employees and inquiries with staff at the Department of Antiquities in Benghazi led nowhere. There is another peculiarity about the robbery: The hole that the robbers drilled through the concrete ceiling was just about big enough to allow a child or a tiny adult through into the vault. How could such a person have carried out the extensive damage to the safes? Perhaps there was another reason why the theft was announced so long after it took place. It has been suggested that after struggling so hard to gain international recognition of their overthrow of the Gaddafi regime, Libya's National Transitional Council were worried that their reputation would be tarnished by admitting to the theft of such important antiquities.

Whatever the reasons for the delay in reporting the incident, it did not change the fact that the valuable objects were missing and that, because there were apparently few if any photographs of the objects, the treasure would be extremely hard to track down. Nevertheless, Francesco Bandarin, UNESCO's assistant director-general for culture, together with a number of Libyan archaeologists, organized a worldwide hunt for the Benghazi Treasure, and Interpol alerted 188 national police forces to be on the lookout for the stolen items. At first these actions seemed to have paid off, as reports came in that a farmer in Egypt had attempted to smuggle a 3-inch-high gold figurine and 503 gold coins through the port city of Alexandria. There were also stories that an unusually high number of classical coins had been appearing on the Benghazi downtown gold market and also on the Egyptian black market. However, authorities were unable to locate the farmer, and it was never discovered whether his items or those sold in Benghazi were actually part of the Benghazi Treasure. Yussuf ben Nasr, director of antiquities for the city, has stated that he believes most if not all the objects have left the country. A worse fear is that the metal objects from the treasure have been melted down and sold. The most serious problem hampering the recovery of the collection is that without detailed illustrations or photographs of the stolen items, it will be almost impossible to prove what exactly belongs to the Benghazi Treasure.

As to the wider issue of the looting of Libya's ancient sites and museums, there appears to some disagreement as to how much damage was done to the country's rich historical heritage during the nine months of hostilities. In August 2011 English-language Indian daily newspaper _The Hindu_ published an article by journalist Vladimir Radyuhin that described mass looting of ancient artifacts in Libya and NATO aircraft bombing of the ancient sites of Leptis Magna and Sabratha. The article also stated that the "plunder of Libya's cultural heritage has been going on since February."[1] The source of this sensational news was a certain Nikolai Sologubovsky, a "Russian expert on Western Asia" also described in the article as a "scholar...orientalist, writer and film maker" who had spent April to July of 2011 in Libya as a correspondent for a Moscow tabloid.[2] Sologubovsky also went on Russian television in August 2011, informing the public that NATO had bombed Libya's ancient sites and that the al-Jamahiriya National Museum in Tripoli had been looted and its antiquities shipped by sea to Europe.

However, in September 2011, a fact-finding mission by UNESCO experts found that there had in fact been minimal damage to Libya's ancient monuments, and no damage at all to Leptis Magna and Sabratha. The lack of major damage was partly because NATO had purposely avoided bombing archaeological sites; indeed, a no-strike list of cultural heritage institutions in Libya had been drawn up before any air strikes took place. So who to believe? Research by Dr. Samuel Hardy of the Conflict Antiquities blog has discovered that Nikolai Sologubovsky was neither a scholar nor an expert on Western Asia, but the official publicist of the Russian Committee of Solidarity with the Peoples of Libya and Syria, which as Hardy says is an "explicitly pro-Libyan dictatorship, pro-Syrian dictatorship lobbying group."[3] Nikolai Sologubovsky obviously has an agenda in spreading stories about mass looting and NATO bombings in Libya, and of course has never provided any evidence to back up his claims.

This disinformation campaign by Sologubovsky does not mean, of course, that looting did not take place in Libya during the rebellion, as the theft of the Benghazi Treasure shows. Unfortunately, the museums and ancient monuments of a country undergoing political and social upheaval will always be at risk of looting and damage, as witnessed in Egypt during the fall of President Hosni Mubarak and in Iraq, after the downfall of Saddam Hussein. Thus museums, auction houses, and art dealers throughout the world need to be made aware that items coming from any country during or immediately after uprisings, like that seen in Libya, may well be looted, and it is their responsibility to check the provenance of such objects carefully. Unfortunately it seems increasingly probable now that the Benghazi Treasure will never be recovered, but its theft does highlight the fact that museums and archaeological sites in Libya are hugely underfunded and a large proportion without adequate security after years of government neglect. For a country with such a rich and varied archaeological heritage, of which the remains of the ancient Greek colonial cities of Cyrenaica are just a part, that is a situation that needs to change soon.

*The Morgantina Treasure and the Looting of Italy*

The Morgantina Treasure is the name given to a 16-piece collection of Greek silverware originating from the ancient settlement of Morgantina in Sicily. The story of this controversial ancient treasure starts around 1979–1980, when looters excavated an area of the ancient site under the very noses of the authorities and made off with a hoard of valuable ancient objects. The treasure was soon smuggled out of Italy and ended up in Switzerland with infamous antiquities dealer Robert Hecht. Over a period of several years in the 1980s Hecht sold the objects to the Metropolitan Museum of Art in New York for around $2.74 million, with the Met announcing its new acquisitions in 1984. Suspecting that the objects had been looted, a prominent archaeologist made numerous requests throughout the following years for an opportunity to view the pieces more closely but was constantly refused by the museum. Eventually the Italian government intervened and the objects were finally returned to Italy in 2010. But why had it taken so long for the Met to admit its mistake, and what does the case of the Morgantina Treasure tell us about the shady world of the black market in Italian antiquities?

The collection of 16 highly ornate silver pieces with gold detail that make up the Morgantina Treasure includes two large bowls, plates, a ladle with a dog's-head handle, pitchers, a cup with two handles, an emblem depicting the mythical sea monster Scylla in sculptural relief, and two distinctive miniature horns, which may at one time have been attached to a helmet. Archaeologists believe that the collection had been hidden inside two decorated kraters (wide, two-handled vessels used in ancient Greece and Rome for mixing wine and water). Such beautifully crafted silverware would have been used for religious ceremonies and symposia (ancient Greek drinking banquets).The fact that the pieces vary in date and style, though they were locally made (probably in Syracuse, a city renowned for its highly skilled silversmiths) and all belong to the third century BC (the Hellenistic period), suggest that the objects were the property of a collector, perhaps the owner of the house in which they were found.

The ancient city of Morgantina is located in fertile hills near the modern town of Aidone, in the province of Enna in central Sicily. The site has been settled at least since the beginning of the late Sicilian Bronze Age (c1270 BC) and was occupied well into the Roman period, up until around 50 BC. The settlement occupied two different sites successively, beginning with the hilltop known as the Cittadella, and from the middle of the fifth century BC the neighboring series of hills called Serra Orlando. Morgantina became established as a significant town in the first quarter of the sixth century BC in the wake of the wave of Greek colonization of many areas of South Italy and Sicily that took place from the eighth to the sixth centuries BC. This Greek area was to become known as Magna Graecia. In 459 BC Sikel leader Duketios (the Sikels were the local indigenous people) captured Morgantina and even managed to defeat a combined army from the powerful Greek cities of Syracuse, in southeast Sicily, and Akragas, on the southern coast of the island.

Although Duketios's control was to be short-lived, perhaps lasting around a decade, it was probably during this period that the site of Morgantina moved to Serra Orlando. At its peak, the second city of Morgantina was an important place, containing around 1,000 occupied house lots and an estimated urban population of around 7,000.

In 396 BC Morgantina was captured by Dionysios of Syracuse, and for the next two centuries it remained under the influence of the mighty Greek city-state of Syracuse. Later, under King Hieron II, who ruled Syracuse and many other cities in eastern Sicily from 270 BC to 215 BC, Morgantina flourished and many of the extant buildings on the site date to his reign. From 262 BC onward, Hieron II had been a faithful ally of Rome, but after his death in 215 BC, during the struggles between the Roman Republic and the Carthaginian Empire (the city of Carthage was located in present-day Tunisia), which constituted the Second Punic War, Syracuse joined forces with Carthage. Morgantina stayed faithful to Syracuse, which fell to the Romans in 212 BC and was sacked by the Roman army the following year. Morgantina was subsequently handed over to the Spanish mercenaries who had fought on Rome's side during the battles in Sicily, and the former inhabitants of the city were sold into slavery. From that time onward Morgantina declined, with a number of public buildings falling out of use and whole residential neighborhoods being abandoned. The latest remains on the site date to around 50 BC, and by the middle of the first century AD the once-flourishing city was no more than a handful of scattered buildings.

Throughout the centuries the ruins of Morgantina gradually disappeared beneath farmland until rediscovered by archaeologists in the modern era. In fact, even the location of Morgantina had been lost in time. In 1955 archaeologists from Princeton University were combing the hillsides around Aidone looking for traces of the ancient site when they began to discover scatters of artifacts and, most important of all, at the top of the Serra Orlando ridge, a small wooden die marked MGT—for Morgantina. It was then they knew that the lost city of Morgantina must lie somewhere beneath their feet. Since 1955 the ancient city has been under excavation by American and Italian archaeologists. The initial excavations were undertaken from 1955 to 1963 and 1966 to 1967 by the Princeton University Archaeological Expedition to Sicily under the joint directorship of professors Erik Sjöqvist and Richard Stillwell of the department of art and archaeology. Excavations continued on the site into the 1970s and beyond; in 1980, Malcolm Bell III, professor of Classical Archaeology at the University of Virginia, took over as director of the Expedition and still directs work on Serra Orlando today.

*6.1. View of Morgantina. Image licensed under the Creative Commons Attribution-Share Alike 3.0 Unported license on Wikipedia.*

More than half a century's work on the remains of Morgantina have revealed some fascinating remains, including a large agora (marketplace) with stoas (ancient Greek covered walk or colonnade) on three sides, a small theater, a granary, various sanctuaries, Classical and Hellenistic houses (many containing mosaics), a bath complex, shops, cemeteries, and roads. Astonishingly, only around a fifth of the ancient site has so far been uncovered.

But where does the Morgantina Treasure fit into all this?

Before the city fell to the Romans in 211 BC, its inhabitants, aware of the fate that awaited Morgantina at the hands of the conquerors, buried their valuable possessions beneath the floors of their houses and other buildings before the legions arrived. But beneath one of these houses, a particularly wealthy inhabitant of the city had concealed something extraordinary. Yet it was not the archaeologists who had painstakingly been investigating the site for years, who were destined to find it. Practically as soon as the archaeologists had begun work on the site in the mid-1950s, local looters known as *clandestine* or *tombaroli* (tomb-robbers) had also began their nefarious activities. In the early years the clandestini used pick axes to break through the walls of ancient houses and tombs in their search for treasures that they could then sell on the black market. But in the 1970s, with the advent of metal detectors, their methods changed, with the result that a number of valuable coin hoards were taken illegally from the site.

In 1980, Malcolm Bell, who was then directing excavations at Morgantina, noticed unauthorized digging taking place on a nearby hill. As the majority of the site is on private land and local officials seemed uninterested in taking action against the clandestini, Bell could do nothing about it. In the months following, Bell began to hear rumors about an exquisite set of silver objects that had been unearthed by local looters, and, although the gossip even described some of the pieces in detail, no substantial information about where the objects had been taken to or by whom emerged. In autumn 1987 Bell was visiting the Metropolitan Museum of Art in New York when he saw a collection of silver on display that struck him as closely fitting the description of the looted objects from Morgantina. Bell subsequently wrote to the museum voicing his suspicions and asking to examine the objects, and at the same time wrote to the Italian authorities informing them of the display. Despite repeated letters to the Met throughout the following years Bell was not given permission to view the objects, and eventually his requests were simply ignored.

In 1996 Bell was asked by the Italian authorities to investigate the structures on the hill where the silver was supposed to have been found. Almost as soon as digging began in 1997 it was obvious to Bell's team that someone had been there before them. The soil was churned up and, when they hit the floors, they discovered two large holes that could conceivably have held the silver treasure seen in the Met. An Italian 100-lira coin minted in 1978 was also found in one of the holes, important evidence for the looting of the site and its approximate date. The discovery of another coin, missed by the looters and minted more than 2,000 years earlier, between 214 BC and 212 BC, fitted with the date when the Romans attacked Morgantina and added weight to the theory that the silver hoard was concealed at this time.

Eventually in 1999 the Met allowed Bell the chance to examine the silver in its collection. This viewing soon convinced him that Morgantina was indeed the origin of the collection, but Bell also noticed something else of interest scratched in Greek onto the surface of two of the pieces. This *graffito* had been translated by museum curator Dietrich von Bothmer as reading "from the war," but Bell believed that it actually read "of Eupolemos" meaning that the objects belonged to a man named Eupolemos. Astoundingly one of the very few family names recorded from Morgantina, on a third-century real estate deed relating to property near the find spot of the silver, is Eupolemos. But was this evidence enough for the Met to admit the origin of the objects and return them to their place of origin? As it turned out, there was another important part of the story that had emerged a few years earlier.

In 1996 a leading Sicilian *clandestini* named Giuseppe Mascara was arrested on charges of antiquities trafficking and, in attempt to reduce his sentence, provided information about the looting of the Morgantina silver. In sworn testimony Mascara described the finding of the silver in 1979, its location, and even details about the decoration on several of the pieces. Silvio Raffiotta, the chief investigating magistrate for central Sicily and a native of Aidone, presented the evidence to the Met, but it dismissed Mascara's claim, citing him as unreliable due to his criminal background. It was after this rebuff by the Met that Raffiotta arranged for Bell's 1997–98 excavations, based on details of the location of the silver provided by Mascara.

Although the evidence against the Met was building up, it took another revelation to fully convince the museum to change its position on the origin of the silver. To reveal details of what this involved, we must look into how the Met obtained the silver in the first place. After the artifacts had been looted from Morgantina sometime in 1979/1980 (probably in two batches, as indicated by the two holes in the house floor) they were sold by two tombaroli, Vincenzo Bozzi and Filippo Baviera, for 110 million lire ($27,000) to Orazio Di Simone, a Sicilian antiquities dealer based in Lugano in Switzerland, who then sold them to U.S. dealer Robert Hecht, Jr., for $875,000. The Metropolitan Museum of Art reportedly bought the silver in two lots from Hecht in 1981–82 for $2.74 million, which again tends to support the theory that the artifacts were looted from the ancient house in Morgantina on two separate occasions. In 1984, the Met announced its new acquisition: a 15-piece set of "some of the finest Hellenistic silver known from Magna Graecia," which it thought could have been made in "Taranto or in eastern Sicily."[1] This reference to both Sicily and southern Italy (Taranto) was uncertain enough to make details of the origins of the silver as vague as possible.

In 2005, when the Met was still stalling over the return of the silver, Robert Hecht was indicted by the Italian government, along with Marion True, the former curator of antiquities at the J. Paul Getty Museum in Los Angeles, for conspiracy to traffic in illegal antiquities. Another co-defendant in the case was Italian dealer Giacomo Medici (also Hecht's business partner) who had been convicted in 2004 of dealing in stolen ancient artifacts. Medici's illegal antiquities operation was believed to be one of the largest and most sophisticated in the world, and when his warehouse space in Geneva Freeport was raided in September 1995, hundreds of pieces of ancient art were discovered; one set of Etruscan dinner plates alone was valued at $2 million. On May 12, 2005, Medici was found guilty and sentenced to 10 years in prison and a fine of 10 million Euros. Evidence taken in the raid on his Swiss premises resulted in the indictment of Hecht and True by the Italian government in 2005.

However, in November 2007, the criminal charges against True were dropped, as the statute of limitations had expired, and her trial ended without resolution. In January 2012 Hecht was acquitted on the grounds that that the statute of limitations on the charges against him had expired. Hecht died in Paris just a few weeks later, at the age of 92.

It is probable that the publicity surrounding the Hecht/True trial finally persuaded the Met to come to a decision about the Morgantina hoard, and in 2006 an agreement was finally reached between the Italian government and the museum. This repatriation agreement allowed the Met joint custody with the Aidone Archaeological Museum of the silver hoard, which would travel between New York and Aidone every four years for exhibit. The agreement also allowed for the Morgantina silver to remain displayed in New York on loan until January 2010. Various other antiquities of Italian origin were included in the repatriation claim, including the Euphronios krater, an almost perfectly preserved early sixth-century BC vessel exquisitely decorated with two scenes, one from the Trojan War and the other depicting Athenian youths arming themselves for battle. The painter of the vase, Euphronios, was a pioneer in the art of red-figure vase painting. Interestingly, the Met had bought this object in 1972 for $1 million from a certain Robert Hecht. The Euphronios krater had been looted the year before by tomb-robbers from an Etruscan tomb in the Greppe Sant'Angelo, near the town of Cerveteri, 30 miles northwest of Rome.

In a related repatriation case, a life-size sculpture known as the Morgantina Aphrodite, or sometimes the Getty Aphrodite (though it is more likely to depict either Demeter or Persephone), was returned by the J. Paul Getty Museum in California to Sicily in 2011. The museum had bought the fifth-century classical sculpture in 1988 for $18 million, apparently unaware that the statue had been looted from a sanctuary at Morgantina in the 1980s. One of the Getty Museum's main suppliers of antiquities during the 1980s was none other than Robert Hecht.

In 2010 the Met returned the 16 pieces of the Morgantina treasure to Italy, and in March of that year the collection went on display at the Palazzo Massimo, Museo Nazionale Romano, Rome. It had taken 30 years for the objects to return to Italy. In December 2010, the treasure finally returned home to Sicily, to the small archaeological museum in Aidone. In May of the following year, the Morgantina Aphrodite was also unveiled at the museum, inspiring the local community with hope for a better future in their economically depressed town. Indeed, the mayor of the town, Filippo Gangi, seemed to voice the hopes of whole community when he said that the return of these valuable artifacts could "trigger an unprecedented economic development" in Aidone.[2]

Because the Morgantina Treasure has been identified and repatriated, we now know the context of the objects and we can go some way toward telling the story behind them. We can connect Eupolemos, the owner of the silver, with the house in which they were found and perhaps even with Syracuse, the place where the objects were made. He may even have been a refugee from Syracuse fleeing the Romans and looking to find safety in Morgantina. The discovery of the buried silver more than 2,000 years later, however, shows that he never found that safety and in all likelihood was killed or enslaved at the time of the Roman assault on Morgantina in 211 BC.

So does the story of the Morgantina Treasure represent hope for the future of Italy's ancient remains? Well, in the wider context of looting in the country, not quite. The question remains: What if it had been clandestini who discovered the initial remains of Morgantina in 1955? The story might have been very different.

Although a number of looted pieces like the Morgantina Treasure have been returned to Italy throughout the past 10 years, this is usually the exception rather than the rule. Italy is particularly rich in ancient tombs, temples, and settlements, and as a consequence there are thousands of clandestini operating in the shadows. In 2010 Italy's Carabinieri art squad announced that they had recovered almost 60,000 pieces of looted or stolen artwork and ancient artifacts worth an astounding $239 million. But is it the local looters who are the problem? The people who actually dig up the loot are usually poor farmers or laborers in need of extra money in order to survive, and ignorant of the worth of their finds. Consequently they sell on their ill-gotten gains to middlemen for a tiny percentage of the actual value of the object. But crucially, the tomb-robbers are the first link in a chain that often leads to the best known art collectors and museums in the world. But it is with the next link in the chain, the middlemen, often locals, but with some knowledge of the items they are dealing with, where the picture of the looting of Italy's ancient heritage begins to cloud over. These middlemen are notoriously hard to identify and prosecute. From the hands of the middlemen the looted objects are spirited out of the country, usually to international traffickers in Switzerland, a country aptly described as the black hole of illegal antiquities. Then the antiquities, complete with faked paperwork, head to London or New York, to private collections, auctions, or museums. As we have seen, once the looted objects have found a home in a museum outside Italy, it is extremely difficult to get them back.

The tragedy is that for every looted ancient object from Italy that appears on the illegal antiquities market, thousands more are destroyed by the looters who smash through the archaeological site, sometimes even using bulldozers, in their zeal for the cash that these objects can bring. The context is gone, and a page torn from the history book of ancient Italy.

## The Sevso Treasure

The Sevso Treasure is a hoard of 14 late Roman silver objects of exceptional quality, reported to be worth more than $200 million on today's market. The astonishing story of this cursed (according to its current owner) treasure is rife with plots and counterplots, suspicious deaths, and back market double-dealing. The treasure was looted from an unknown Roman palace or villa sometime in the 1970s, and appeared in London in the early 1980s with an export license from Lebanon, later shown to have been forged. The silver was subsequently purchased by the Marquess of Northampton and in 1990 was on display in New York ready for auction later the same year. But before this could happen, the governments of Lebanon, Hungary, and Yugoslavia lodged legal claims to it. In 1993, however, an American court rejected these claims and ruled that the Marquess was the legal owner of the controversial silver. This decision caused an uproar in Hungary, whose claim, backed by a number of experts, was that the hoard had been discovered in their country in 1978 by a quarry worker (later found hanged) and illegally exported. In 2007 it was sensationally reported that another 200 silver objects from the original hoard were known to exist, but their whereabouts remain unknown. Today the Sevso Treasure, left without any secure provenance and tainted by its dark history, is regarded as unsalable.

The name of the Sevso Treasure derives from an inscription on one of the silver plates, which reads:

> Hec Sevso tibi durent per saecula multa
> Posteris ut prosint vascula digna tuis

> Let these, oh Sevso, yours for many ages be,
> Small vessels fit to serve your offspring worthily

Small vessels? The inscribed silver "Sevso" plate is 27.5 inches in diameter and weighs almost 20 pounds, and the combined weight of all 14 pieces comes in at a staggering 154 pounds or so. The lavishly decorated silver tableware that makes up the Sevso Treasure was accompanied by a large copper cauldron, within which it was discovered. As luck would have it, this huge cauldron had preserved its contents from oxidation, so the silver was in excellent condition, although much of it showed signs of use. According to Dr. Marlia Mango of the University of Oxford, the treasure dates from between AD 350 and AD 450, though some Hungarian scholars, among them Dr. Zsolt Visy, of the University of Pécs, maintain that the objects were all manufactured within the fourth century AD. Interestingly, radiocarbon dating of soot on the copper cauldron dates it to sometime between AD 140 and AD 410, but with an error margin that could extend it as late as AD 610. This latter date is when Dr. Mango believes the treasure was buried.

The treasure consists of a collection of four large plates, five ewers (pitchers), two buckets, a cosmetic casket, an amphora, and a basin, all elaborately decorated with hunting, feasting, and mythological scenes; images of everyday life; and intricate geometric forms. Unusually for a hoard, there were no spoons or coins, items that are often found together with sets of Roman tableware. The Sevso plate itself, also known as the Great Hunting Dish, is one of the earliest pieces in the collection, probably dating from the mid- to late fourth century AD. The Hunting Dish has at its center a medallion decorated with scenes of hunting and an outdoor banquet, and the Achilles Plate, at 28.3 inches in diameter the largest object in the Sevso hoard, depicts the legend of Achilles. The spectacular Meleager Plate is decorated with a central medallion showing the Greek hero Meleager after killing the Calydonian boar, flanked by the huntress Atalanta and four other Calydonian Hunters. The rim of this huge vessel is decorated with a frieze showing a range of mythological scenes including the Judgment of Paris and the story of Perseus and Andromeda.

Other impressive pieces from the Sevso Treasure include a large drinking vessel known as the Hippolytus Jug, which has two beautifully crafted handles in the shape of leopards and a ewer 1 1/2 feet tall and embossed with a Dionysiac procession. This vessel was probably used for serving wine while other vessels in the assemblage were used for eating, drinking, and for washing hands. Tantalizingly, most archaeologists agree that these 14 objects are only part of what was once a much bigger hoard.

Dr. Zsolt Visy divides the 14 objects in the Sevso Hoard into two groups, those with repoussé decoration (embossing or pressing shapes into metal), namely the Achilles plate, Meleager plate, amphora, Dionysiac ewer, Hippolytus ewer, two Hippolytus buckets, and the casket; and those decorated using a black inlay called niello, these being the geometrically decorated plate, Hunting plate, two geometrically decorated ewers, a ewer decorated with animals, and the basin. She also believes that within these two main groups only a few can be assigned to the same workshop or craftsman. Dr. Mango also considers the objects to be the work of a number of different craftsmen, and thinks that they were manufactured in various parts of the Roman Empire and collected throughout a long period. A number of the objects, including the amphora, Dr. Mango believes, may have been made in the eastern Mediterranean region, perhaps Constantinople, whereas others may have come from a workshop in Thessaloniki, in northern Greece.

Scholars are of the opinion that "Sevso" was either a Roman general or an extremely wealthy Roman client, probably of non-Roman background, judging by the origin of his name, and the silver probably a lavish wedding gift. Interestingly, the Chi-Rho sign (an early Christian monogram, formed by superimposing the first two letters of the word "Christ" in Greek: Chi [X] and Rho [P]) used to signify the beginning and the end of the inscription on the Hunting Plate shows that Sevso and his family may well have been Christians, or at least believed in the efficacy of this Christian symbol. And that, really, is all we know of Sevso;

*7.1. View of Lake Balaton. Image by Nobli. Licensed under the Creative commons Attribution-Share Alike 3.0 Unported license on Wikipedia.*

the rest is conjecture. But what of the extraordinary journey of the treasure itself?

The truth is that no one knows for sure (or is telling) where the treasure was before the end of 1980. According to the Hungarian version of events, the story begins in the town of Polgárdi, Fejér county, central-western Hungary. Sometime in 1978, a

22-year-old quarry worker named József Sümegh was carrying out excavation work at the stone quarry, which lies near the village of Kőszárhegy, northeast of Lake Balaton, when his shovel hit something metallic. When he investigated further he found a large, grime-encrusted copper vessel containing a hoard of silver objects, but due to the filth covering the artifacts, he didn't realized the extraordinary nature of what he found. What Sümegh did next with the treasure is a mystery, though he may have hidden it in his family home in Polgárdi. Later Sümegh apparently took as many as six (accounts vary) of the objects to sell at the flea market near Budapest airport. Someone at the market seems to have realized the value of the objects, as they later turned up in Vienna, a center of the antiquities trade, in the possession of Halim Korban, a Lebanese antiquities dealer, and his partner, Anton Tkalec, a Yugoslav Serb coin dealer.

A few months later Sümegh apparently left his job at the quarry and moved to Budapest. He returned home some weekends, but told his family little about his new life, though it was obvious from his expensive clothes that he had somehow come into money. At the beginning of 1979, Sümegh went to fulfill his national-service duty at the army barracks in Papa, to the northwest of Polgárdi. Around this time he is believed to have hidden the treasure in a hole in the floor of an old wine cellar close to Polgárdi. Years later, stories surfaced that Sümegh had shown the treasure to a few of his friends, some of whom had held and examined it; one, István Strasszer, described a heavy box decorated with birds on its top. Others stated that Sümegh had told them of finding a buried silver treasure that comprised about 200 pieces and that he had sold some pieces of the collection to a Lebanese dealer.

Whatever the truth of these statements, in November 1980, a silver ewer from the treasure appeared in London, probably via Halim Korban, and was sold to a consortium called the Art Consultancy, which seems to have included Rainer Zietz, a German-born art and antiques dealer, and Peter Wilson, recently retired as chairman of Sotheby's. Wilson was a colossal figure on the London art market and the center of a network of antiquities dealers. He was also, to say the least, an interesting character. Credited by many as the one person responsible for creating the modern Sotheby's, during WWII Wilson was employed by MI6 with the code number "007," where he became friendly with Ian Fleming, Navy Intelligence's liaison officer with MI6. According to Wilson's own story he was part of the inspiration for Fleming's James Bond character. In his book, *Sotheby's: The Inside Story* (Random House, Westminster, Md., 1997) author Peter Watson mentions that Wilson was also suspected of being a Soviet spy and that he retired as chairman of Sotheby's soon after Sir Anthony Blunt, an art historian and former MI5 officer, was exposed as a member of the Cambridge Five, a group of Soviet spies working for the Soviet Union from 1934 to at least the early 1950s. This is an interesting theory, and Wilson did have connections with members of the Cambridge Five, though there is no direct evidence he was ever a Soviet spy.

Be that as it may, Peter Wilson subsequently arranged to have the ewer from the treasure examined at the British Museum, where it was cleaned and revealed to be a rare and valuable piece of fourth- or fifth-century Roman silver. So as not to arouse suspicion Korban brought further objects from the treasure to London one or two at a time, and it seems these were bought by Peter Wilson and the Art Consultancy.

At around the same time (December 1980), in Hungary, the body of József Sümegh was found hanging from the rafters of the disused wine cellar. The verdict was suicide. The treasure, which had apparently been buried close by, was gone, leaving only a hole in the ground. Throughout the next couple of months, two more of Sumegh's friends were apparently found dead in the area. According to Peter Landesman in his 2001 *Atlantic Monthly* article on the Sevso case, one of Sumegh's coworkers at the quarry had died after eating poisoned cheese, and another was found hanging by his neck in a forest. Were these deaths coincidences? The Hungarian police seemed to think so, as their investigations could not officially link the three deaths.

However, in 1993 a prisoner named József Lelkes told a tabloid newspaper that József Sümegh had indeed discovered the Sevso Treasure and that three other people who knew of his discovery had died in mysterious circumstances. In 1990, a decade after the events, Bela Vukan, the police officer in charge of the Hungarian investigation into the Sevso Treasure, decided to follow up on local rumors that Sümegh's death had not been suicide, but murder connected to the Sevso Treasure. Vukan carried out investigations into the supposed suicide and came to the conclusion that Sümegh could not have hanged himself with his military belt, as the official investigations had stated. Vukan believes that Sümegh was murdered and his body placed in the wine cellar to obscure the origins of the treasure.

Peter Landesman's *Atlantic Monthly* article also contained further sensational nuggets of information about Sümegh's connection with the treasure. Landesman describes meeting Zoltan Fodelmesi, the principal of the local school, and a keen coin collector who often traded with József Sümegh. Fodelmesi told Landesman that Sümegh had shown him the treasure and that he (Fodelmesi) had advised the young man to take it to the National Museum in Budapest. Ominously Fodelmesi also confessed that even 20 years after seeing the mysterious Roman silver he was still afraid for his life. Knowledge of the treasure was a dangerous thing, he said. Landesman also mentions meeting József Sümegh's younger step-brother Ishtevan, who informed him that together with József's other step-brother, Attilla, they had helped clean one of the pieces of the treasure with sandpaper (!). Ishtevan also claimed that after József found the treasure he was visited by Russian and Hungarian officers, and that he believed that the military was connected with his half-brother's death.

The Sevso Treasure was meanwhile appearing in London piece by piece via Halim Korban and Anton Tkalec, and in 1981 Wilson and lawyer Peter Mimpriss (of the firm Allen & Overy) persuaded Spencer Compton, the Marquess of Northampton, to take part in the purchase as an investment through the Art Consultancy. Northampton was told that the Treasure would be far more valuable if complete, and so in the early years of the 1980s he spent around $16 million acquiring what he believed to be the full set.

Northampton's plan was to resell the silver later through the agency of Peter Wilson. He told police in 1990 that he was unaware of its exact origin, but believed Korban and Tkalec when they told him that it had been found in the Tyre and Sidon regions of Lebanon. By 1983, the year of Wilson's death, Northampton had obtained 10 pieces of the treasure and offered them for sale to the wealthiest museum in the world, the J. Paul Getty Museum in Los Angeles, for $10 million. However, when the Getty examined the Lebanese export certificates accompanying the silver it found them to be fake. Seemingly unperturbed by this, Peter Mimpriss, by now Northampton's lawyer, arranged for new Lebanese documents, via his agent in Beirut, Ramiz Rizk. But the Getty naturally became suspicious and backed out of the deal.

Throughout the next few years Northampton acquired four more pieces of the treasure and by 1990 was the sole owner of the entire 14-piece collection. At a news conference in New York in February of the same year, Sotheby's announced the existence of a fabulous silver treasure worth $70 million that had been found in the 1970s in "what was once the province of Phoenicia in the Eastern Roman Empire"[1] (in other words, modern Lebanon). According to Sotheby's, the Lebanese Embassy in Switzerland had authenticated the licenses used to export the treasure from Lebanon. On February 9, 1990, London newspaper *The Independent* published a number of articles about the Sotheby's auction, which stated that, although the provenance was uncertain, the Sevso hoard was believed to have been found in either Lebanon or Eastern Europe. Soon after, on February 14th, Sotheby's put the treasure on display in New York, in preparation for a proposed auction in Switzerland. But before the auction was announced, Sotheby's had notified the 29 countries whose territory had once lain within the borders of the Roman Empire of the impending sale of the Sevso Treasure, inquiring whether the pieces were recorded as stolen property. This is when the trouble started. On February 15th the Republic of Lebanon put in a demand for the return of the treasure, followed by claims from the Federal Republic of Yugo-slavia (soon to become Croatia) and, almost a year later, Hungary.

Prolonged legal proceedings followed, as each country car-ried out extensive investigations into the treasure and attempted to uncover evidence that the valuable silver had been in fact dis-covered in its territory. However, before the case came to trial, Lebanon withdrew its claim, mainly because of the fake Leba-nese export licenses. Finally, in November 1993, the New York Court of Appeals rejected the claims of both Hungary and Croa-tia, finding them "without merit," and ruled that the tainted sil-ver should be returned to the Marquess of Northampton.

If the Marquess was the innocent dupe in the Sevso affair he has always claimed to be, then it is obvious that his legal advisors at the time, Allen & Overy, were not looking out for his interests. Left with a priceless yet unsalable collection of Roman silver, in 1999 Northampton decided to sue Mr. Mimpriss and his London law firm, Allen & Overy, for damages in relation to the advice they gave him during the purchase of the silver, charging them with "fraud and conspiracy to defraud."[2] The case was eventu-ally settled out of court, with the Marquess receiving a reported $28 million in compensation.

After the court case nothing was heard of the Sevso Treasure until September 2006, when Bonham's announced a private exhi-bition of the pieces to take place on October 17th of that year. Rumors were that the Marquess was again trying to offload the silver, and indeed he was quoted by the online version of the English newspaper *The Guardian* on October 17, 2006, as say-ing he "hopes" the Sevso Treasure will be sold, and that it has "cursed" his family.[3] But putting the treasure back in the public eye did not attract the buyer Northampton hoped for; instead it brought a renewed claim of ownership from Hungary in the form of a letter from its Ministry of Education and Culture. The letter stated that the treasure could not be sold, as it was the property of the Hungarian state, and that Hungary "maintain[s] our claim of title to it and will take all possible legal measures pursuant to this."[4] The matter of the Sevso Treasure was even brought up in the House of Lords, in answer to searching questions about the Bonhams exhibition put by Colin Renfrew, Baron Renfrew of Kaimsthorn, a prominent archaeologist and senior fellow of the McDonald Institute for Archaeological Research in Cambridge, UK. Nevertheless, the exhibition went ahead, and although the Sevso Treasure was not sold, no legal claim to ownership was made by Hungary.

But does Hungary—or, for that matter, Croatia—have a legitimate claim to the Sevso Treasure?

Croatia's claim to the treasure was partly based upon information given by phone to a journalist named David Keys, who worked for *The Independent* newspaper. Keys would not reveal his source, but in March 1990 *The Independent* ran a story that stated that the treasure had been discovered in the 1970s by Yugoslav troops at a military instillation near the town of Pula, on the southern tip of the Istrian Peninsula in what is now Croatia. The silver had then been smuggled out of the country in a diplomatic pouch. At the New York trial Yugoslavia produced allegedly eyewitness testimony to support its claim to the treasure in the form of Anton Cvek, a retired secret policeman from Pula. Cvek testified that in May 1961 he had seen pieces of the Sevso Treasure at a military base near the village of Barbariga, around 13 1/2 miles northwest of Pula. He also stated that he had seen further pieces at a house in Barbariga the same day. Cvek's testimony was supported by another retired secret policeman from Pula called Ivan Kauric, who stated that he been with Cvek at Barbariga and had also seen the treasure.

Unfortunately for the Yugoslav/Croatian claim, it was later revealed that Kauric had changed his story a number of times. For example, when interviewed by Croatian authorities on three separate occasions between 1990 and 1992, he had repeatedly stated that he had no knowledge of any silver treasure from Barbariga. Cvek also later stated that he was not sure if the silver in Barbariga was actually the Sevso Treasure. But Cvek's greatest inconsistency was his description of the silver plates that he had seen as the size of dinner plates—obviously much smaller than the huge examples in the Sevso hoard. In June 1991, a report by the Croatian Ministry of Internal Affairs admitted that, after a lengthy investigation, it could find no evidence that the Sevso Treasure had been found in Yugoslav/Croatian territory.

Hungary appears to have a much more watertight claim on the Sevso Treasure. Retired detective sergeant Richard Ellis, formerly with Scotland Yard's Art and Antiques Squad, who carried out extensive investigations into the provenance of the silver, believes the Hungarians have the strongest case. Indeed, there appears to be a substantial amount of hard evidence for the legitimacy of the Hungarians claim. One piece of this evidence appears on the central medallion of the Hunting Plate from the collection, in the form of an inscription bearing the word "Pelso," next to a body of water. Pelso is the Roman name for Lake Balaton, just a few miles away from where József Sümegh supposedly discovered the treasure. Another link with the Sevso Treasure is an exquisitely decorated silver tripod, in Hungary's National Museum in Budapest, interpreted by Hungarian archaeologists as a folding table (called a quadruped). This object was found in 1878 near Polgárdi, and Zsolt Mrav of Hungary's National Museum is convinced that there is a close connection between the quadruped and the Sevso Treasure, due to similarities in decoration and date. (The object is thought to date to the middle/second half of the fourth century AD.)

Scientific evidence also seems to support Hungary as the provenance of the treasure. In her article "Contributions to the Archaeology of the Seuso Treasure" (in *Antiquaries Journal*) Dr. Zsolt Visy states that mineralogical analysis using electron microscopy of soil samples taken from the Meleager Plate matched soils in the area of the village of Szabadbattyán, 18.6 miles from Lake Balaton. Furthermore, Dr. Visy states, X-Ray Diffraction Analysis of the soil encrustations on the copper cauldron that contained the treasure and soil taken from the pit in the wine cellar showed that they had the same mineral composition. Therefore, he reasons, they can be considered as materials from the same soil environment. In the same article Dr. Visy refers to a definite connection between József Sümegh's discovery of the Sevso Treasure and his murder in the wine cellar. Hungary's use of the soil samples from the wine cellar and József Sümegh's murder in support of its claim to the Sevso Treasure are of vital importance, and we will return to them later.

The majority of the evidence for the Hungarian case was presented in a Channel 4 (UK) special edition of their popular archaeology TV show *Time Team*. The show, entitled "The Mystery of the Roman Silver," aired in December 2008 and contained interviews with many of the major players in the Sevso drama, though not Lord Northampton, and the show was not allowed to film the treasure itself, which was then held in a vault at Bonhams in London.

If the treasure did originate in Hungary, what was its history and why was it buried? Dr. Visy believes that in light of the apparent reference to Lake Balaton on the Hunting Plate, the discovery of the Roman quadripod near Polgárdi, and the results of the soils sampling, Sevso must have been the wealthy owner of one of the large Roman villas located around the shores of the Lake. Dr. Visy suggests the villa in question was the huge example near the town of Szabadbattyán (from where the soil samples were taken). Excavations at the villa site in the 1990s revealed traces of burning and destruction, dating to around the end of the fourth century, which could be interpreted as signs of an attack, possibly by barbarian invaders. Could the Sevso Treasure have come from this villa and have been concealed at the time of this attack, to be unearthed 1,600 or so years later by József Sümegh? This scenario certainly sounds plausible.

However, not everyone is convinced by the evidence put forward by Hungary in support of its claim. In terms of the "Pelso" inscription on the central medallion of the Hunting Plate, Dr. Marlia Mango notes that another neighboring inscription reads "IN(N) OCENTIUS," probably the name of the horse illustrated next to it. The "PELSO," inscription, Dr. Mango believes, may relate to the dog seated above the inscription, rather than the water illustrated, which appears more like a river or stream than a lake.

There are also questions surrounding the soil sample evidence that seemingly puts the origins of the Sevso Treasure in Hungary. At the 1993 New York trial both Croatia and Hungary were asked to provide soil samples from various parts of their countries to establish whether their soil matched ancient encrustations found on pieces of the treasure. Due to the fact that Croatia delayed its submissions and constantly changed the samples it wished to submit, it was forbidden by the court from using them to support its claim. The court came to the same decision about Hungary, prohibiting it from using a soil sample from the wine cellar where the treasure was allegedly kept. Why was this? At the trial, police officer Bela Vukan admitted that there were no witnesses who claimed to have seen the treasure in the wine cellar. Much more seriously for the Hungarian case was the fact that the former owner of the cellar told the Hungarian authorities that the indentation in the floor of the cellar was in fact where a wine vat had been placed for many years. This is interesting, as in the 2008 *Time Team* show about the treasure, Bela Vukan still pointed out the indentation in the wine cellar as the place where the cauldron containing the silver had once been hidden.

In fact, when Dr. Anna Bennett of the Conservation and Technical Services carried out analysis of the encrustation on the cauldron, the results showed that it had not been buried in the earth at all, but concealed in a limestone environment, such as a natural cave or a chamber.

The New York trial (well summarized in Kate Fitz Gibbon's *Who Owns the Past?*) revealed a number of facts that do not reflect well on Hungary's claim to the Sevso Treasure. In September 1990 József Sümegh's father informed the Hungarian authorities under oath that after seeing the publicity in Hungary surrounding the possibility of a great Roman treasure being found in the country he thought there must be a connection with the death of his son, who was an enthusiastic collector of old coins and medals. Mr. Sümegh urged the Hungarian authorities to investigate the matter, and it was after this that the case of József Sümegh's suicide was reopened.

At the trial there were a number of witnesses called on by Hungary's lawyers who claimed to have seen pieces of the treasure at Sümegh's family home in the late 1970s. One of the witnesses was someone we have already met: István Strasszer. Strasszer, a stonemason, testified that he had seen several pieces of the silver at Sümegh's home in 1978 or 1979 and identified the cosmetic casket specifically. At a previous interview with Hungarian authorities, Strasszer had produced a drawing of the casket, giving its dimensions. A model replica of the casket based exactly on Strasszer's measurements was constructed and presented at the trial. Unfortunately for the Hungarians, this model was a fraction of the size of the real Sevso casket. Another witness from Polgárdi who claimed to have seen the treasure was Joszef Harmat, who testified that he had seen the copper cauldron on a shelf in Sümegh's home. Harmat identified the cauldron from a picture of it in a fully restored state, the result of extensive restoration work began in 1988. However, in the late 1970s, when Harmat claimed to have seen it, the cauldron in its unrestored state would have been unrecognizable, and Harmat would not have been able to identify it.

Another witness called by Hungary was retired schoolteacher Istvan Fodelmesi, who seems to be the same person as Zoltan Fodelmesi, the local school principal who Peter Landesman describes meeting in his *Atlantic Monthly* article. In 1991 Fodelmesi had been questioned twice by Hungarian authorities and swore under oath that he had never seen the Sevso Treasure in Sümegh's possession; in fact, he denied any knowledge of the treasure at all. However, two weeks before the New York trial, Fodelmesi suddenly changed his story to the version he told Peter Landesman. Conspicuous, by their absence, from those Hungary called as witnesses at the trial were members of József Sümegh's family living at the house when the treasure was allegedly being kept there. Perhaps this was because the Hungarian authorities had previously taken sworn statements from every member of Sümegh's family, and they all denied having seen any silver either in the house or in the possession of József.

This is all the more curious when we remember József Sümegh's younger step-brother Ishtevan telling Peter Landesman about using sandpaper to clean a piece of the treasure. Furthermore, Ishtevan would have been only around 7 years old at the time of this alleged incident.

All of this underhand dealing seems to bear out the statement that the record of the 1993 trial "is rife with allegations of witness interference and fears (real or not) of government retaliation."[5] What appears to be witness manipulation on Hungary's part does not of course rule out Hungary as the source of the Sevso Treasure, but it does cast an uneasy shadow over their claim. All the evidence points to the fact that the tragic suicide of a 24-year-old man was transformed by the Hungarian authorities into a murder connected with the Sevso Treasure, in an attempt to provide a back story for its discovery in their country. Since the New York Court of Appeals rejected its claim in 1993, Hungary has provided no new evidence nor taken any further legal action regarding the Sevso Treasure. As it stands at the moment, Hungary's claim to the treasure remains plausible but unproven.

One of the main difficulties proving a provenance for the Sevso silver is that, although there have been a number of discoveries made of late-Roman high-quality silver tableware, very few pieces are of a similar size. Furthermore, those finds that are comparable have been discovered mainly in the Western provinces of the Roman Empire. Neither Hungary nor Croatia has any record of material similar to the Sevso Hoard ever being found on their soil.

One similar piece to the Sevso Hunting Plate is the Great Dish from the Mildenhall late-Roman Treasure, a stunning hoard of highly decorated fourth-century Roman silver tableware found in Mildenhall, Suffolk, in the east of England (see Chapter 8). The Great Dish is 23.8 inches in diameter and is elaborately decorated with the face of the sea-god Oceanus at its center, surrounded by scenes detailing the worship and mythology of Bacchus. Other items in the Mildenhall Treasure are also decorated with pagan mythical scenes, and some of the spoons in the collection bear the Christian Chi-Rho monogram.

The closest parallel for the Sevso Hunting Plate is the Kaiseraugst Plate, part of the Kaiseraugst Treasure, a rich, fourth-century hoard discovered in a Roman frontier fort on the river Rhine, east of Basel in Switzerland. The Kaiseraugst Plate, also known as the Achilles Plate, is 23.2 inches in diameter and is beautifully decorated with a central medallion showing scenes from the early life Achilles. The Kaiseraugst silver hoard appears to have been amassed over a period of time by high-ranking Roman officers, as the name "Marcellianus" appears on 13 of the items, and the items includes gifts from two Roman emperors. The treasure was probably hidden away in advance of an attack by the Alamanni, an alliance of Germanic tribes living around the Upper Rhine River. Inscriptions on a number of the items show that many of the silver pieces were made in Thessaloniki, northern Greece, also a possible place of manufacture for the Sevso Treasure. As with the Sevso Treasure, the motifs depicted on the silver tableware from Kaiseraugst are hunters, landscapes, and scenes from Greek mythology.

Another ceremonial gift from a Roman emperor to a civic or military official is the magnificent Missorium of Theodosius I. This huge, elaborately decorated Roman silver plate, at 29 inches in diameter, even larger than the Sevso Hunting Plate, was probably crafted in Constantinople in AD 388 for the 10th anniversary of the reign of Theodosius I, Roman Emperor from AD 379 to AD 395, and the last to rule over both the eastern and the western halves of the Roman Empire. The Missorium was part of a hoard of silver objects discovered in 1847 in Almendralejo, close to Mérida, formerly the Roman city of Emerita Augusta, in western-central Spain.

The relatively large amounts of rich late-Roman hoards discovered in the UK (covered in Chapter 8), combined with the fact that the Sevso hoard first appeared in London, has prompted some researchers, including Lord Renfrew of Kaimsthorn, to bring up the question of a possible British origin for the treasure. The Mildenhall Treasure has already been mentioned, but rich hoards from Thetford, Water Newton, and elsewhere in the UK are also relevant. The Roman silver hoard known as the Water Newton Treasure was discovered near the fortified Roman garrison town of Durobrivae, at Water Newton in Cambridgeshire, in the east of England. Some of the pieces from this fourth-century collection are inscribed with Chi-Rho monograms, and the ornately decorated silver jug resembles the ewers from the Sevso hoard. Another rich hoard containing silver tableware, is the mid- to late-fourth-century AD Roman hoard from Thetford, Norfolk, eastern England, which also yielded exquisite Roman gold jewelry.

Also important in the context of late-Roman silver hoards is the Corbridge Treasure, found in the River Tyne at Corbridge, once the Roman fort and town of Coria, in Northumberland, northeast England. A magnificent late-fourth-century silver tray, known as the Corbridge Lanx, from this hoard depicts a shrine to Apollo, with Apollo's twin sister, Artemis (Diana), and Athena (Minerva) also in attendance. The tray was probably manufactured somewhere in the Mediterranean, North Africa, or Asia Minor. No other pieces from the hoard have been located, but a number were sketched or described when they were originally found in 1735, and at least one of them bore Christian symbols. In 1993 the British Museum bought the Lanx from the Duke of Northumberland for a fee reported to be in excess of £1.8 million.

Despite these examples, however, without further evidence it is a fruitless exercise to guess at the provenance of the Sevso Treasure, which could in reality be anywhere in the vast Roman Empire.

In March 2007, *The Art Newspaper* claimed to have had access to documents from the 1980s that revealed the existence of previously unknown pieces of the Sevso Treasure. In an article entitled "The Silver Missing From the Seuso Hoard?" Cristina Ruiz alludes to a document from Halim Korban addressed to Guernroy Ltd., a division of the Royal Bank of Canada in Guernsey, in the Channel Islands. This document mentions "remaining silver objects from the hoard (187 silver gilt spoons, 37 silver gilt drinking cups, and 5 silver bowls)"[6], seemingly indicating that these objects were originally part of the Sevso Treasure, but had been split up from the 14 known pieces purchased by Lord Northampton.

Another document cited by *The Art Newspaper* was a letter dated April 6, 1987, from another Guernsey-based concern,

Ferico Trust Ltd., to Ramiz Rizk, the previously mentioned associate of Lord Northampton's lawyer, Peter Mimpriss. The letter, sent to a PO box in Lebanon, mentions that Rizk has "agreed to obtain export licenses for the remainder of the hoard which we understand to be various cups and spoons, at a price under half the cost of the first three licenses."[7] There were also rumors of the existence of two other silver plates, one with an engraved Chi-Rho in the center and the other known as the Constantine Plate, which showed a portrait of Constantine I (Roman Emperor from AD 306 to AD 337) in the center, that might be part of the Sevso Treasure. However, despite the documents and the speculation, Lord Northampton's lawyer Ludovic De Walden said in a statement to *The Art Newspaper,* that there was "no direct evidence now or before of there being any pieces forming part of the Sevso hoard beyond the 14 pieces."[8]

Later that same year came more speculation regarding the Sevso Treasure. In July 2007, the Croatian weekly newspaper *Globus* and the Hungarian weekly *Budapester Zeitung* carried a story claiming that Hungarian-born American businessman George Soros was buying the Sevso Treasure from Lord Northampton and donating it to the National Museum in Budapest. However, the reports were soon denied both by representatives of Soros in New York and by Lord Northampton, who stated categorically that the he was not selling the treasure to Soros. Nothing has been heard of this alleged sale since.

Although most museums in the world would consider the remarkable pieces of Roman silver in the Sevso hoard an important centerpiece of their collection, the lack of a recognized provenance, the forged export licenses, and the court claims by Croatia and Hungary mean that museums (or private buyers, for that matter) are unlikely to acquire the silver any time soon. The end result of the controversial and sad tale of the Sevso Treasure is that these spectacular examples of Roman craftsmanship will remain locked away in a bank vault, inaccessible for study and for all intents and purposes lost to the world.

Roman Treasures From England:
The Hoxne Hoard and the
Mildenhall Treasure

The Roman occupation of Britain lasted from AD 43 until about AD 410. During this period various people, from soldiers to wealthy citizens, from thieves to craftsmen, buried their wealth in the soil, either for safe-keeping, as a votive offering to the gods, or, if the objects were obtained illegally, as a temporary hiding place. However, it is often not possible to know the individual circumstances in which some hoards were deposited, and in these cases we can only glean information by comparison with other, similar hoards. Roman hoards can contain tableware in gold, silver, bronze, or pewter, gold jewelry; precious stones; gold, silver, bronze, or copper coins; inscribed silver or gold plaques; iron or bronze weaponry; and scrap metal. Hoards from the first two centuries of relatively stable Roman rule are more likely to be deposits of wealth in a safe place (akin to a modern bank), and items were probably added to and taken out of the hoards during this period.

However, a significant amount of hoards date to the last half century or so of the Roman period in Britain, a time of political instability in the country and of frequent raids by Picts, Scots, and Saxons. With such an uncertain future, it was natural for people to hide their wealth in a secret place, though obviously not everyone was able to return to collect their cache. Many extremely rich hoards were deposited during the tumultuous last decades of Roman Britain, such as those from Hoxne and Mildenhall (both in Suffolk, in the east of England), the rich jeweler's hoard from Thetford in Norfolk, and the huge cache of sliced-up silver from Traprain Law, near Haddington, East Lothian, Scotland. The latter example shows a regard for the value of the metal rather than the objects in the hoard and may represent loot from a battle or a raid. The Water Newton Hoard, from Cambridgeshire in the east of England, is a hoard of fourth-century silver that provides vital evidence for Christianity in Roman Britain. Indeed, the items in the hoard have been described as the earliest group of Christian liturgical silver ever found in the Roman Empire and indicate the presence of a small private chapel in the area where the treasure was found.

Coin hoards are especially common from Roman Britain, with more than 1,200 examples known and more being discovered each week with the increase in the popularity of metal detecting. Because the coins depict the current Roman Emperor, they can be used to date the hoard in which they are found fairly securely, though only the earliest possible date for the hoard (obtained from the oldest coin) can be known for sure; the latest date is more difficult to determine, as coins may have been in use for decades after they were minted. Coin hoards can give us vital information about Romano-British history, and one particularly important example is the Chalgrove Hoard, discovered in 2003 about 10 miles southeast of Oxford. The hoard consists of bronze and silver coins dating from AD 251 to 279, and includes an extraordinary coin of a previously unknown Roman emperor named Domitianus, a usurper emperor whose reign only lasted a few weeks.

The Shapwick Hoard of 9,262 coins, discovered in 1998 in Shapwick, Somerset, in the southwest of England, provides a vast date range of coins from 31 BC to 30 BC up until AD 224. The collection includes 260 *denarii* (small silver coins) of Mark Antony from 31 BC, and two rare coins that depicted Manlia Scantilla, the wife of Didius Julianus, Roman emperor for nine weeks during the year AD 193. Didius Julianus was murdered in June 193, soon after these coins were minted.

One of the largest Roman coin hoards ever discovered was unearthed near Frome in Somerset, as recently as April 2010, and consists of an astonishing 52,503 silver and bronze coins dating from AD 253 to AD 305. Fascinatingly, experts believe that the massive thin pot that contained the hoard was too fragile to have been used to carry the coins and would need to have been smashed to access the treasure. This fact points to the possibility that the Frome Hoard was a ritual offering to the gods, perhaps by an entire community, judging by the vast amount of coins in the collection.

### ≈The Hoxne Hoard

The Hoxne Hoard is the largest cache of late Roman gold found anywhere in the Roman Empire. Discovered by a metal detector-ist in Suffolk, in the east of England, in 1992, the incredible collection contains 14,865 late-fourth-century and early-fifth-century Roman gold, silver, and bronze coins, and 200 items of silver tableware and gold jewelry. The hoard amounts to a total of 7.7 pounds of gold and 52.4 pounds of silver, and its current value is estimated at around $4.3 million. As the finder reported his discovery immediately, the cache was professionally excavated by archaeologists and conserved soon afterward, so the vital context of the objects and their condition were preserved. Thanks to the coins in the hoard, we know that the items were deposited in the early fifth century AD, right at the end of the Roman occupation of Britain, which tells us a great deal about an important period in the history of the country when Roman rule was breaking down and a new age was approaching.

On November 16, 1992, retired gardener and amateur metal detectorist Eric Lawes was scanning a field southwest of the village of Hoxne in Suffolk, on the lookout for a hammer that the local tenant farmer, Peter Whatling, had lost. While searching for the hammer, Lawes stumbled upon a cache of metal objects, including gold chains, silver spoons, and coins, some of which he dug out and packed into two carrier bags before notifying Whatling of his spectacular find. Lawes and Whatling decided to report the discovery to the landowners, Suffolk County Council, who, due to the importance of the finds, promptly organized an excavation of the site. The excavation, undertaken by Suffolk County Council Archaeology Service (SCCAS), took place the next day in secret in case the location of the hoard became known and the site looted.

But somehow the story got out, and on November 19th the British tabloid *The Sun* splashed the story across its front page along with a picture of Lawes and his metal detector, and a claim that the treasure was worth £10 million. In characteristically obtuse fashion, the paper also announced the prize of a metal detector to anyone who could answer the question "Who built Hadrian's Wall? Hadrian, Barretts or Wimpey?" Meanwhile, the excavated treasure from Hoxne, along with Peter Whatling's missing hammer, was taken to the British Museum. The unwanted publicity surrounding the find forced the British Museum to hold a press conference on November 20th announcing the discovery, which served to dampen the interest of the newspapers, and permitted the curators at the museum to begin to categorize and clean the artifacts from the hoard. Further excavations in and around the find spot took place in September 1993, and also in 1994 due to illegal metal detecting around the site.

On September 3, 1993, a coroner's inquest declared the Hoxne Hoard a treasure trove. In other words, the treasure was deemed to be of unknown ownership and to have been hidden with the intention of being recovered later. In November the Treasure Trove Reviewing Committee valued the hoard at £1.75 million (today £2.66 million, or $4.3 million), which was paid to Eric Lawes as finder of the treasure. Lawes generously shared his reward with farmer Peter Whatling (which it is now a legal requirement to do). The Hoxne Hoard is now in the British Museum, and the most important items are on display in a Perspex reconstruction of the oak chest and inner boxes in which they were originally deposited.

The excavations at Hoxne found that the hoard had been contained inside a rectilinear feature, interpreted as being the decayed remains of a wooden chest that once held the objects. Other fragments recovered by the archaeologists, including box fittings such as hinges and locks, showed that the finds had been carefully organized into separate wooden boxes and fabric containers inside the larger oak chest. Such meticulous packing was one of the reasons why the objects were so well preserved when recovered. Archaeologists also uncovered an undated post hole, which may once have held a wooden post that served as a marker for the burial spot of the hoard.

The fabulously rich contents of the Hoxne Hoard include 569 gold coins, 14,191 silver coins, and 24 bronze coins. The gold coins (all *solidi* of about 4.5 grams of gold per coin) date to the reigns of eight different emperors between Valentinian I (reigned AD 364–75) and Honorius (reigned AD 395–423). Most of the coins in the hoard were silver *siliquae* (small, thin, Roman silver coins produced from the fourth century onward), of which there were a staggering 14,212. There were also 60 silver *miliarenses* (large silver coins introduced by Constantine I) and 24 bronze *nummi* (low-value coins). The coins from the Hoxne Hoard provide extremely helpful dating evidence for its deposition; the oldest coin in the collection is a well-worn miliarensis of Constantine II (Roman emperor from AD 337–340) and the latest two siliquae of the usurper Constantine III (reigned AD 407–408). Thus the hoard must have been buried sometime after AD 407–408, and, although we do not know how long existing coins remained in circulation, it is unlikely to have been for more than perhaps 30 years, giving a probable date for the deposit of the hoard of not later than AD 450.

Just as important for giving us information about the Hoxne Hoard are the mint marks stamped on many of the coins, which identify where in the Roman Empire they were minted. Fourteen different mints are represented in the Hoxne Hoard: Trier, Arles, and Lyon (in Gaul—modern France); Aquileia, Milan, Ravenna, and Rome (Italy); Siscia (in modern Croatia); Sirmium (in modern Serbia); Thessaloniki (Greece); and Constantinople, Nicomedia, Cyzicus, and Antioch (in modern Turkey).

The hoard contains 29 pieces of stunning gold jewelry: a gold body chain, six chain necklaces, three finger rings, and 19 bracelets. One of the bracelets bears the inscription "VTERE FELIX DOMINA IVLIANE" ("Use [this] happily lady Juliane"), which obviously indicates the name of the owner, Juliane. The body

chain from the hoard is a fascinatingly rare object, which would have been passed over the shoulders and under the arms of the wearer, to be fixed in place by two clasps. There are two decorative clasps where the chains join; on the front one there is an amethyst surrounded by four garnets and four empty settings, which once probably held pearls (which have since decayed), and on the back a gold coin of Emperor Gratian (reigned AD 375–383) set into a gold frame. The small size of the Hoxne

*8.1. The gold body chain from the Hoxne Hoard. Image by Mike Peel* www.mikepeel.net. *Licensed under Creative Commons Attribution Share Alike 2.5 on Wikipedia.*

body chain suggests it would only fit a very slim young woman or an adolescent girl. Interestingly, the gold frame of the coin was a reused pendant, perhaps a century old when incorporated into the elaborate body chain, suggesting a family heirloom.

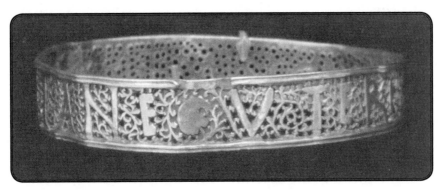

*8.2. Juliane bracelet from the Hoxne Hoard. Image by Fae. Licensed under Creative Commons Attribution Share Alike 3.0 on Wikipedia.*

The collection of magnificent silver objects from the hoard consists of 78 exquisitely crafted spoons, 20 gilded and decorated ladles, four extremely rare pepper-pots, five bowls, two vases, nine toilet implements (toothpicks and ear-cleaners), and two padlocks from now-decayed small wooden caskets. A number of the spoons are decorated with a Christian monogram cross or Chi-Rho symbol, and one is engraved with the common Christian phrase "VIVAS IN DEO" ("May you live in God"). One of the gold necklaces also bears a Chi-Rho symbol. Such inscriptions must certainly attest to the Christian beliefs of their owners and add important evidence for Christianity in late Roman Britain.

One set of 10 silver spoons from the hoard are inscribed with the personal name "Aurelius Ursicinus." Although this is the most common name in the hoard, there is no evidence that this was the name of the owner of the objects. One of the most spectacular of the silver items is the handle in the form of a prancing tigress with niello (a black compound of sulfur with silver, lead, or copper, used for filling in engraved designs in silver or other metals) stripes and a long tail, which seems to have been purposely detached from a large vessel before deposition. But perhaps the most celebrated item in the whole hoard is known as the "Empress" pepper pot, a silver pepper or spice container of about 3 inches in height in the form of a hollow female half-figure. The figure's clothing, jewelry, and intricate hairstyle are gilded and beautifully crafted. There is an internal disc in the base of the figure that can be rotated to be completely open for filling with pepper or other spices, partially open for sprinkling on food, or completely closed. Although initially believed to represent a Roman empress, specialists now believe that the "Empress" pepper-pot depicts a wealthy Roman aristocrat, perhaps even the Lady Juliane who owned the inscribed gold bracelet from the hoard. Pepper was an incredibly rare but popular commodity to the Romans; it was not grown anywhere in their Empire, so it had to be imported from India, across the Indian Ocean and up the Red Sea to Egypt, and then across the Mediterranean to Italy and Rome.

As with many other hoards, including the Staffordshire Hoard (see Chapter 11), there is no evidence for contemporary buildings and certainly no rich Roman villas in the immediate vicinity of the location of the Hoxne Hoard. The closest Roman occupation in the area is at Scole, where a Roman Road known as Pye Road (the modern A140) crosses the River Waveney, about 2 miles to the northwest of the find spot. Five miles southwest of the location of the Hoxne Hoard there is evidence for a Roman settlement at Stoke Ash, also located on the Pye Road. Both Scole and Stoke Ash have been suggested as the location of the Villa Faustini, a site mentioned in the Antonine Itinerary; a written description began in the third century AD describing the Roman Empire's major roads and stations upon them, which includes 15 routes in Britain. The Villa Faustini was obviously an estate owned by a man named Faustinus, but where exactly it was located and who Faustinus was are unknown.

The Hoxne Hoard is not a completely isolated find. In 1781 laborers discovered a lead box close to the River Dove in Eye, about 2 miles to the south west of Hoxne. The box contained about 600 Roman gold coins dating between the reigns of Valens and Valentinian I (reigned together AD 364–375) and Honorius (AD 393–423). Unfortunately the coins have long since been scattered among various private collectors and are almost impossible to trace. Whether this hoard was related to the Hoxne cache or not, it does perhaps suggest something else. Dr. Peter Guest, senior lecturer in Roman archaeology at Cardiff University, and author of *The Late Roman Gold and Silver Coins from the Hoxne Treasure*, has noted the concentration of late Roman hoards in East Anglia and suggests in the book "an entrenched cultural tradition of deliberately and permanently abandoning precious metal in the ground."[1] In this hypothesis, hoards in the area would have been votive deposits, although Guest has also suggested an alternative theory that argues that the Hoxne Hoard was deposited because the objects in it were used as part of a gift-exchange system, which broke down when the Romans left Britain.

Another possibility is that the Hoxne Hoard represents the loot from a robbery, concealed by the thief, who was, for whatever reason, unable to return to recover it. However, the simplest explanation for the presence of the Hoxne Hoard is that it was deposited by a wealthy family in an isolated spot for safekeeping after AD 407 in uncertain, even dangerous times as Roman soldiers were departing from Britain. Perhaps the family had to leave Britain in a hurry during this turbulent period, which is why they were not able to retrieve their treasure—or at least not all of it. Researchers have noted that some common types of Roman jewelry are absent from the hoard, and the types of large silver tableware objects found in the Mildenhall Treasure (discussed later in this chapter), which a wealthy Roman family would surely have owned, were also missing. Fabulously rich as it is, the Hoxne Hoard may only represent part of an even greater treasure.

### The Mildenhall Treasure

Discovered in Suffolk 1943, at the height of WWII, the hoard of objects known as the Mildenhall Treasure is a collection of late-Roman silver tableware perhaps unequalled in the Roman

Empire. The cache of 34 exquisitely decorated items was acquired by the British Museum in 1946 but little is known of its ownership or its origins. Even the treasure's discovery has an element of mystery, exemplified by Roald Dahl's short story about the hoard, first published in 1946. With such an air of uncertainty surrounding the discovery and origins of the hoard, it is perhaps not surprising that tales have grown up questioning its Romano-British origin and even suggesting that it had been secretly smuggled into Britain from the Mediterranean.

On a freezing cold January day in 1943 Gordon Butcher was deep plowing a field belonging to a farmer named Fred Rolfe, at West Row, 2 miles northwest of the market town of Mildenhall in Suffolk, when he hit a large metal dish. Knowing he had found something out of the ordinary but unsure of what to do, Butcher went to get Sydney Ford, an agricultural engineer from whom he had rented the plowing equipment and someone who also happened to collect local antiquities. The two men excitedly dug together as the snow fell and had soon unearthed a large number of objects, including dishes, bowls, and spoons. They then put the objects into a sack and carried it to Ford's workshops at West Row, where Ford carefully examined each piece and Ford's workmen helped to straighten pieces that had become bent. After extensive cleaning Ford put various items of the collection of what he believed to be pewter on display on his sideboard. The man who first discovered the artifacts, Gordon Butcher, now drops out of the story for a while, though whether he was paid off, as stories circulating at the time suggest, has never been proven.

Sometime in 1946 a Buckinghamshire doctor and amateur antiquarian named Dr. H.A. Fawcett visited Ford, from whom he had bought antiquities in the past, and managed to view the items from the hoard. Realizing the importance of the objects, Fawcett persuaded Ford to loan him a few items to take to the British Museum for analysis. Experts at the British Museum subsequently identified the objects as Roman silver, and Fawcett persuaded Ford to declare the find to the authorities. The treasure was then confiscated by the police, who launched an inquiry into the matter. In the summer of 1946 an inquest was held, and on July 1st the hoard was declared treasure trove and became the property of the Crown. Although newspapers published articles quoting the value of the hoard at a huge (for the time) £50,000 ($76,523), Ford and Butcher were only given a reward of £2,000 to share between them ($3,061). This was far from the full market value, perhaps because Ford had not reported the find correctly and had also delayed doing so for a long period after its discovery. After the inquest the British Museum acquired the treasure, and it remains there to this day.

Roald Dahl, the English author of *James and the Giant Peach, Charlie and the Chocolate Factory,* and many others, wrote a short story about the hoard, "The Mildenhall Treasure," which was first published (under the title "He Plowed up $1,000,000") in the *Saturday Evening Post* magazine in the United States in 1946. After reading about the story in a newspaper, Dahl visited Mildenhall and apparently interviewed a number of people involved in the case, including the plowman, Gordon Butcher, to whom he later sent a check for half of the money he made from selling the piece to the *Saturday Evening Post.* The story was later published in Dahl's short story collection *The Wonderful Story of Henry Sugar and Six More.*

The Mildenhall Treasure consists of 34 silver items, including serving platters, plates, dishes, bowls, goblets, ladles, and spoons. Some of the pieces are spectacularly decorated. The Great Dish, as it has become known, is without doubt the most spectacular and well known of all the pieces in the Mildenhall Treasure; in fact, it could be said to symbolize the treasure itself. The object is a circular platter (serving dish) almost 2 feet in diameter and weighing more than 18 pounds. Its beautifully executed relief decoration divided into three concentric zones, the outer of which features Bacchic revellers, including Bacchus himself, Hercules, the goat-footed god Pan, several dancing Maenads (the female followers of Bacchus), and Satyrs. The narrow inner decorative band illustrates Nereids (sea-nymphs), Tritons, and other mythical and natural marine creatures; and the face of a bearded sea-god (Neptune or Oceanus) with dolphins in his hair stares out from the center of the dish. Two smaller plates are decorated in the same style, one showing Pan playing his pipes and a Maenad playing the double flute, and the other decorated with a dancing Satyr and a dancing Maenad; these plates must surely have been made in the same workshop as the Great Dish.

*8.3. The Great Dish from the Mildenhall Treasure in the British Museum. Image by JMaill. Licensed under Creative Commons Attribution Share Alike 3.0 on Wikipedia.*

A number of the beautifully crafted flanged (projecting flat rim, collar, or rib on an object) bowls in the collection are also decorated with such Bacchic scenes. One particularly attractive example shows a mixture of Bacchic imagery and both mythical and real animals. An exquisite covered flanged silver bowl has a high-domed lid (actually made later than the bowl) decorated with Bacchic masks between scenes of Centaurs attacking wild animals. The lid also has a knob formed from a small statuette of a young seated Triton blowing a conch shell. Fascinatingly, this third-century AD bowl is the oldest in the Mildenhall Treasure, and the only object in the hoard whose area of manufacture (Gaul [modern France]) is known for certain. The eight spoons discovered in the Mildenhall Treasure represent three (or perhaps four) groups or sets, why the owner did not deposit the complete sets with the hoard is not known. Three of these exquisitely shaped spoons are the only obvious evidence for Christian beliefs in the hoard, having the Christian Chi-Rho symbol inscribed between Alpha and Omega (the first and last letters of the Greek alphabet, an appellation of Christ) in their bowls. Another two spoons are inscribed with personal names; one reads "PAPITTEDO VIVAS" ("long life to Papittedus"), the other "PASCENTIA VIVAS" ("long life to Pascentia"). This evidence for Christianity in the hoard contrasts with the pagan nature of the decoration on many of the objects, especially the Bacchic scenes.

In terms of dating the Mildenhall Treasure, we are not lucky enough to possess the late-Roman coins present in the Hoxne Hoard and a number of other Roman hoards. In the absence of coins we have to rely on stylistic similarities to other Roman artifacts to date the cache. The style and decoration of the artifacts point to a fourth-century AD date for the Mildenhall Treasure, which is supported by the handful of Christian inscriptions, compared to the more predominantly pagan character of the decoration on the objects. This is what would be expected, as Christianity was slowly gaining influence in Roman Britain in the fourth century, and signs of the new religion would have co-existed with the pagan beliefs of the majority of the population. It has been suggested that the owner of the Mildenhall Treasure was a wealthy Christian, perhaps one Lupicinus, a Christian *Magister militum* (master of soldiers), a high-level commander who was sent to Britain in AD 360 by Roman Emperor Julian the Apostate to defend the frontier from attacks by the Picts (from eastern and northern Scotland) and the Scots (from Ireland). Lupicinus was recalled to Gaul two years later and arrested, and it has been suggested that he or members of his family may have buried the Mildenhall Treasure for safekeeping in Britain when he left. If the treasure did indeed belong to Lupicinus, then one can assume he brought it with him when he came to Britain, so the Gaulish origin of the covered bowl may make some sense. However, why was the treasure deposited in a field apparently in the middle of nowhere?

But had the field where the Mildenhall Treasure was found always been empty? In 1932 traces of what had probably been a small, fourth-century Roman villa were discovered 30 yards from the find spot of the hoard. Finds from the site included pottery and the remains of a hypocaust (heating) system. Could the Mildenhall Treasure be connected to the occupants of this villa? Archaeological work in the area of West Row since that time has uncovered evidence of late-Roman settlement in the form of features such as ditches, pits, and post holes, and finds such as ceramic building material, pottery, copper alloy coins, and animal bone. At Beck Row, to the northeast of West Row, a large Roman barn and maltings (malt house) were discovered, signifying considerable agricultural activity in the area. This evidence of Roman activity in the vicinity of the finds pot of the Mildenhall Treasure certainly shows that it was not an isolated field during the Roman period. Nevertheless, so far there is no evidence for the grand residence that would be expected for the owner of such rich objects as those in the Mildenhall Treasure.

At the time of the 1946 inquest into the treasure general opinion was that the objects found by Butcher and Ford were of much too high a quality to have originated or have been used in provincial Roman Britain. There were even theories that the treasure had originally been looted from sites in Italy or North Africa during WWII and flown to the U.S. military airbase at Mildenhall, where it was then buried close to the base's perimeter, which is indeed in the very area where the hoard was supposedly discovered. There is no evidence to prove or disprove this story, though are we to believe that both Butcher and Ford were involved in this conspiracy? Anyway, more recent discoveries of Roman hoards such as the Hoxne Hoard and the Water Newton Treasure show that high-quality Roman gold and silver were in use in Roman Britain, and there is no reason to doubt the same for the Mildenhall Treasure. Despite this fact, however, the circumstances of the discovery of the Mildenhall Treasure leave many questions unanswered.

One problem with Butcher and Ford's story of the discovery while plowing is the lack of significant damage to any of the artifacts, especially the Great Dish. If the objects were hit by a plow and then hurriedly dug up using a shovel, then there would surely be some signs of this in the form of scratches, dents, or cracks, though to be fair there are dents on the four flanged bowls, which could have been caused by the plow. Another problem is that Ford and Butcher changed their story about when and where the hoard was discovered on more than one occasion. Ford initially claimed to have found the treasure in January 1942 on land owned by Fred Rolfe, but later said that he had in fact discovered the cache in January 1943 while walking across a recently plowed field. Ford subsequently changed his story again and went back to his original account. More worrisome, when a thorough excavation of the find spot initially identified by Ford was undertaken in September 1946, nothing at all was found — not a single Roman artifact, nor even a trace of the original hole in which the treasure was supposedly buried. One can only assume that the archaeologists were digging in the wrong place, and that they had been misdirected by Ford.

A further point to consider is Ford's delay in reporting the find, ostensibly because he thought the objects were made of pewter and need not be reported. But if Ford was a collector of antiquities, surely he could tell the difference between pewter and silver. C.W. Phillips, who took part in the unproductive excavation of the West Row site in 1946, was sure that Ford and Butcher's relatively small reward for finding the treasure was a nominal amount due to the fact that the authorities saw so many inconsistencies in their account of the discovery of the treasure.

Some interesting local rumors have been circulating about the treasure for decades. The first of these concerns landowner Fred Rolfe, who told of a local tradition that there was treasure buried in the field on his land where the Mildenhall Treasure was found. The late Tom Lethbridge, who took part in the 1946 excavation in Rolfe's field, mentions the fact that in 1922 representatives of a firm of solicitors from the nearby town of Bury St. Edmunds paid Sydney Ford's father £20 for permission to dig in the field where the Mildenhall Treasure would later be found. The men informed Ford's father that they had received a letter from a man living overseas giving information about a treasure buried in the field so many paces from the "meadow gate."[2] Whatever the truth of this story, the men did not find anything, but could Sydney Ford have been searching the area for this lost treasure when he found the Mildenhall cache? Had he found other pieces of the treasure before the main hoard of 34 objects and not told anyone? Strangely enough, Oliver Cromwell is said to have hidden treasure "chests of silver" in or near three round barrows (burial mounds) known as Three Hills, at Warren Hill on the edge of Mildenhall Woods. During excavation of one of these barrows in February 1866, local people descended on the site after hearing the rumor that one of Cromwell's treasure chests had been uncovered. The rumor was false, but the excavations did reveal a female skeleton, pieces of red deer antler, and Bronze Age pottery. The mounds were destroyed soon after the excavations.

Another local rumor, but with more substantial evidence to back it up, is that originally the Mildenhall Treasure was larger but Ford kept some of the pieces back from the authorities, and later sold them or kept them somewhere in his house. Incredibly, evidence to support this story did not emerge for more than half a century after the find was originally announced. In December 2002, 94-year-old Mildenhall resident Jack Thompson, who had helped clean the treasure at Ford's workshop just after it had been discovered, went to see the set of replicas of the hoard on display at the Mildenhall Museum and noticed something was missing. Mr. Thompson told Dr. Colin Dring of the Mildenhall Museum about a missing silver goblet, which he remembered cleaning, and described as being 5 inches high with intricate decoration and four legs. Interestingly, subsequent research by Dr. Dring discovered that the goblet was not listed on any inventory of the finds after they were made public and was not included as part of the treasure trove inquest of July 1946. The British Museum also stated that it had no record of the goblet.

There were further astonishing revelations a month later, in January 2003, when the British Museum announced that after studying an old photograph showing the Mildenhall Treasure it was convinced that there was another piece missing from the collection in its possession. The photograph, taken some time between 1942 and 1946, shows Jack Ford, Sydney's son, in the West Row house with the treasure on display on the sideboard behind him. Experts from the museum identified a vessel in the photograph that is not part of the museum's collection from Mildenhall and stated that they had no idea what had happened to it. Where are these missing pieces, and are they the only artifacts missing from the Mildenhall Treasure? There are many unanswered questions concerning just about every aspect of the Mildenhall Treasure: its place of origin, the contents of the original hoard, its time and place of discovery, and the whereabouts of the "lost" pieces. Unfortunately as the hoard was found more than 65 years ago during WWII, or possibly even earlier, these questions are unlikely to be answered. Sydney Ford was certainly keeping secrets about the treasure; perhaps one day surviving relatives of Mr. Ford will be traced who can shed some light on these secrets and help in our understanding of the Mildenhall Treasure.

# The Treasures of Pompeii

**C H A P T E R 9**

In August of AD 79 Mount Vesuvius, in the Bay of Naples, along the southwestern coast of Italy, erupted violently, destroying the Roman cities of Pompeii and Herculaneum, and burying them under 13 to 20 feet of ash. Thousands of people in the cities, in the surrounding countryside, and along the seashore were killed as they tried to escape or barricaded themselves inside their houses. Excavations of sites in the area from the 18th century onward have revealed the bodies of some of the city dwellers, frozen in time and preserved in their original context along with their possessions, which they tried so desperately to hang on to. A number of treasure hoards both small and large have been recovered from the ruins of these cities of the dead, and two of the most important are those from the wealthy villas of Boscoreale, just to the north of Pompeii, and Casa del Menandro, in Pompeii itself. These hoards of silverware, jewelry, and coins seem to have been hurriedly secreted away just as the vast clouds of ash from Vesuvius loomed over Pompeii, and tell us a tragic but fascinating story of Roman life in the first century AD.

The cataclysmic eruption of Vesuvius in AD 79 resulted in a number of mostly isolated deposits of valuable items in Pompeii and Herculaneum and in the surrounding countryside. Such deposits include silver plates, mirrors, and cups; silver coins; an exquisite statuette of Indian ivory; and gold armlets, rings, and earrings. Because these objects were sealed in context by the volcanic ash from Vesuvius, many of them can be precisely dated and give us extraordinary insights into Roman art and the lifestyles of the people who owned them. These generally isolated discoveries, however, are easily eclipsed by the treasure hoard discovered in 1895 in the Villa della Pisanella at Boscoreale, a plush suburb on the slopes of Vesuvius, a mile north of Pompeii.

9.1. *Plaster casts of three bodies from the area of Porta Nocera, Pompeii. Courtesy of Wikipedia.*

The Boscoreale area was home to a number of aristocratic country villas, most notably the exceptionally well-preserved Villa Boscoreale, justly celebrated for its elaborate frescoes and mosaics. The Villa Pisanella was discovered in 1868 by Modestino Pulzella, but proper excavation of the site did not begin until 1895. In April 1895, during excavations of the *torcular-ium* (a room housing a wine/oil press), archaeologists discovered a hoard of treasure that had apparently been stashed in an empty cistern below the room, presumably at the time of the eruption of

Vesuvius. The hoard included a leather purse containing a cache of more than 1,000 gold *aurei* (a coin valued at 25 silver denarii), the latest of which dates to AD 78, a few pieces of gold jewelry, some bronze objects, and 99 exquisite pieces of silver tableware.

The remarkable collection of fine silver vessels, which were manufactured between the end of the first century BC and the beginning of the first century AD, included a hand mirror illustrated with a scene showing the Greek myth of Leda and the Swan; a fine silver wine vase; the "Africa Dish," a partially gilded silver vessel exhibiting high-quality applied, repoussé, and engraved decoration showing a female bust wearing an elephant hide and surrounded by various symbols (scholars believe this may be a portrait of Cleopatra, or her daughter Cleopatra Selene II, or an allegorical personification of Africa); two silver skyphoi (two-handled, deep wine-cups) known as the Boscoreale Cups of the emperors Augustus and Tiberius; and a pair of extraordinary wine cups, embellished with gold, and illustrated by skeletons labeled with the names of renowned tragic and comic poets and famous Greek philosophers. One of these vessels is inscribed "Enjoy life while you have it, for tomorrow is uncertain." This maxim became horribly relevant for the inhabitants of the Villa Pisanella, as is graphically illustrated by the many skeletons found at the site of those people who did not manage to escape the disaster in time.

On the whole, the silver collection from the Villa Pisanella suggests a prosperous Roman family; indeed a number of the silver pieces in the hoard are so elaborate as to suggest they were used for display rather than use. Some of the silver pieces (for example, the Boscoreale Cups) showed significant signs of wear, indicating that they were heirlooms. As everywhere in the area at the time of the eruption in AD 79, the family was taken completely by surprise and seems to have attempted to hide their valuables in the villa as quickly as possible. Unfortunately, any further interpretations are difficult because of uncertainties about the size and exact context of the hoard, due to the fact that almost as soon as the objects were discovered, they were sold and exported out of Italy.

The exact series of events at the time of the discovery at the Villa Pisanella is unclear. We know that the Villa itself was located on private land belonging to Vincenzo da Prisco, who sold the treasure and various other finds from the site to an antiquarian named Canessa, who exported the finds and put them on the market. Subsequently, the Louvre was asked if it was interested in the objects, but found the price too high, and so the treasure was subsequently broken up and began to be sold off as single items. (The Africa Dish was sold to the British Museum, for example.) At this stage, philanthropist and collector Baron Edmond James de Rothschild (1845–1934) stepped in, and agreed to buy the hoard and donate it to the Louvre, on the condition that it go on permanent display there. De Rothschild acquired the various pieces that had been sold individually, except for the Africa Dish, which the British Museums refused to part with, and retained six pieces of the treasure for himself, including the Boscoreale Cups. These cups were later donated to the Louvre by a descendant of the baron, and now the entire Boscoreale Treasure is displayed in the Louvre.

Thirty-five years after the discovery of the Boscoreale Treasure, another astounding hoard was unearthed, this time in Pompeii itself. The treasure of the Casa del Menandro was discovered by Professor Amedeo Maiuri in December 1930, during the course of the excavation of the Insula of the Menander, a major city block in Pompeii. The house is thought to have belonged to Quintus Poppaeus Sabinus, a wealthy relation of the Emperor Nero, due to an inscription on a seal found in one room of the house bearing the name "Quintus," and two more found in another room bearing the name "Sabinus." However, this connection is far from proven.

The treasure itself was found in two boxes in a wooden chest in a small cellar under the atriolum (small hall/ante-room) of the bath-suite of the house. What remained of the box (traces of wood and a small lock) in the upper part of the chest contained pieces of gold and silver jewelry and a number of coins; the lower level held 118 pieces of well-preserved silver plate of varying dates and styles, wrapped in cloth. Consequently, this treasure actually forms two separate hoards. The first hoard, from the upper level of the chest, consists of 20 pieces of gold jewelry: two small necklaces, three pairs of earrings, two arm rings, two hairpins, a bulla (ornamental pendant), 11 rings, and a small ball of fine gold wire (probably used for repairing the other pieces of jewelry). Some pieces of the jewelry (the earrings, necklaces, and rings) were decorated with pearls and various precious stones.

9.2. *Pompeii with Vesuvius in the background. Image by Sören Bleikertz. Licensed under Creative Commons Attribution Share Alike 3.0 on Wikipedia.*

Discovered along with the jewelry were a rather modest collection of 46 coins, 25 of which were Republican *denarii* (one dating from 152 BC, the rest from 90–32/1 BC), eight silver Imperial denarii, and 13 *aurei* of Nero and Vespasian. The latest coins in the hoard were three aurei of Vespasian, dated to AD 78–9, thus dating the whole deposit in the upper box to AD 78–9 at the latest, the time of the eruption of Vesuvius. It is important to note that all of the coins need not have been deposited hurriedly at the time of the eruption, but may have been put there earlier as savings or even as a source of ready cash.

The silver plate in the lower level of the chest is of vital importance in terms of finds of Roman first-century silver, as it represents the only large hoard of such items found in a secure, undisturbed archaeological context, and the latest date for its deposit has been given by the eruption of Vesuvius. The hoard, which is the largest collection of roman silver plate ever discovered, also included the only surviving complete Roman dinner service for eight people. The discoverer of the hoard, Professor Maiuri, divided the table plate into drinking silver, which included a scyphus (large drinking cup) decorated with scenes showing the labors of Hercules, and a large saucepan with a figured handle; eating silver, which included large plates, pepper pots, sauce pots, and spoons; show silver, which included a phiale (a shallow cup resembling a saucer) decorated in gold with a female personification of a walled city (Tyche); and toilet silver, which included decorated mirrors and washing bowls.

Some important questions emerge about the two hoards at Casa del Menandro. Who deposited these treasures in the chest, and are the jewelry and the silver plate contemporary? To begin with the jewelry, the question of ownership is rather more complicated than it may first appear. Were these pieces personal possessions or a collection hoarded for their monetary value? And what about the coins? Professor Maiuri has suggested the collection of jewelry could have belonged to one of the ladies of the house, though there are too many items to have been worn all at the same time. There are, however, pieces of jewelry in the collection that would have been used by men and children, which may suggest the pieces were a family collection. Professor Maiuri also believed the Casa del Menandro, and consequently the hoards found within it, belonged to high-class Romans of significant wealth. However, Kenneth S. Painter, in his monograph, *The Insula of the Menander at Pompeii – Volume IV: The Silver Treasure,* suggests that the house could well have belonged to a local magistrate.

Painter also raises some other interesting points about the Casa del Menandro Treasure in his monograph. For example, he questions the connection between the owner of the jewelry hoard in the upper level of the chest and the owner of the silver plate. How do we know they were the same person? Due to the dates of the artifacts in the two hoards, the silver plate may even have been placed in the chest as early as AD 60, well before the eruption of Vesuvius, and therefore deposited there for some other reason. If so, then the owner of the rather modest collection of jewelry and the owner of the fine collection of silver plate may have not have been the same person. In fact, they may not have even been of the same class.

The hoard from the Casa del Menandro is similar in size and grandeur to the Boscoreale Treasure, though the former has a more complete set of eating silver while the latter has more drinking silver.

There is another fascinating hoard of Roman silver with similarities to both the Casa del Menandro and Boscoreale Treasures. This is the Hildesheim Treasure, unearthed near the city of Hildesheim, Lower Saxony, Germany, in October 1868. The Hildesheim hoard is the largest collection of Roman silver ever found outside the frontiers of the Roman Empire, and consists of around 70 exquisitely crafted pieces of solid silver tableware, including cups, goblets, mixing bowls, serving dishes, plates, table implements, and a small folding three-legged table. We do not have the eruption of Vesuvius to help in the dating of this hoard, but it was probably deposited sometime in the late first century BC or early in the first century AD, either by a Roman commander campaigning in Germany or perhaps as booty captured from the Romans by a Germanic tribe. Interestingly, one theory is that the Hildesheim hoard may have been stolen from Roman commander Publius Quinctilius Varus in AD 9 at the famous Battle of the Teutoburg Forest, in the German state of Lower Saxony, where an alliance of Germanic tribes ambushed and destroyed three Roman legions.

The Boscoreale and Casa del Menandro Treasures are significant today in terms of the light they shed on the lives of well-off members of Roman society living in the area of Vesuvius at the time of its catastrophic eruption. The hoard from Casa del Menandro is of prime importance due to its discovery during a professional archaeological excavation; thus the position and description of each object have been meticulously recorded. Because of this we have a reliable source of information about the people who deposited the objects and the society in which they lived. But it is important to remember that not every precious item found in hoards sealed by the ash of the volcano was necessarily deposited at the time of the eruption. Some pieces, such as the Casa del Menandro silver, may have been secreted away earlier and for another reason, and therefore have a very different story to tell.

## Lost Treasures of Afghanistan

The 2,000-year-old Bactrian Gold is one of the largest hoards of gold ever discovered, and the story behind its loss and rediscovery is as extraordinary as the treasure itself. The Bactrian Gold, a cache of gold jewelry, ornaments, and coins from northern Afghanistan, was excavated in the late 1970s, only to go missing during the chaos caused by the foreign occupation and civil war that were to grip the country for the next two and a half decades or so. During this tumultuous period the National Museum of Afghanistan was looted several times, resulting in a loss of 70 percent of the estimated 100,000 objects on display. Had the same fate overtaken the Bactrian Gold? Or had it been taken to Moscow by the Soviets, or smuggled out to Europe or the United States, or—worst of all—melted down? It seemed impossible that such important and priceless artifacts could vanish without trace. During the 1990s and up until the U.S. invasion of Afghanistan in 2001, the Taliban had made repeated attempts to recover the treasure, but had been unsuccessful. Then in June 2004, an announcement was made that a number of supposedly lost treasures of Afghanistan had been recovered, and the astonishing story behind the Bactrian Gold was revealed to the world.

*10.1. Gold earrings from Tillya Tepe. Licensed under Creative Commons Attribution-Share Alike 3.0 on Wikipedia.*

The Bactrian Gold (also known as the Bactrian Treasure or Bactrian Hoard) was excavated in 1978 near the oasis town of Sheberghan, in northern Afghanistan, by a Soviet-Afghan archaeological team led by the Greek-Russian archaeologist Viktor Sarianidi. The team discovered the artifacts, which date to around the first century BC in six simple chambers inside a burial mound under a hill known as Tillya Tepe (the Hill of Gold), near the Oxus River in what was once Bactria. Tillya Tepe was in fact the earth-covered mud brick ruins of a fire-worshippers' temple dating from the Iron Age (1500 BC–1300 BC). The historical region of Bactria was located between the mountains of the Hindu Kush and the ancient Oxus River, in what is now part of Afghanistan, Uzbekistan, and Tajikistan. Bactria became especially important between c600 BC and c AD 600 as a crossroads where international trade and cultural exchange between East and West took place. In fact, the Silk Road, an ancient network of trading routes that ran from China all the way to the Mediterranean, with connections to Siberia, India, and Persia, ran straight through the area.

The fabulous objects that were uncovered at Tillya Tepe accompanied the burials of six wealthy nomads (possibly Sakas — Asian Scythian nomads), probably a chieftain and five female members of his household. The burials were arranged in typical steppe nomad fashion, with the prince in the center, and the graves of the five women in a ring around his tomb. Although the coffins, clothes, and skeletons had mostly rotted away, thousands of pieces of gold jewelry, funeral ornaments, and personal belongings survived intact. The male burial in the group, Tomb IV, was a chieftain who was accompanied by a rich array of grave goods including turquoise-studded daggers and sheaths, two bows, a long sword, a leather folding stool, the skull and bones of a horse (the remains of a horse sacrifice), and an Indian medallion that, in the opinion of Véronique Schiltz, a French archaeologist with the National Center for Scientific Research in Paris, bears one of the earliest impressions of Buddha.

Another of the burials, known as Tomb VI, was that of a 25- to 30-year-old woman, who was accompanied by a thin hammered gold leaf crown with detachable peaks, making it suitable for storage during travel. Clasped in her left hand was a gold coin of Parthian King Gotarzes I (95 BC–90 BC), and a silver coin had been placed in her mouth — in keeping with the Greek tradition of paying a toll to Charon to be taken across the Styx into the underworld. Sarianidi believed this young woman to be a nomadic princess. Tomb II at Tillya Tepe held the remains of a woman in her 30s wearing a signet ring depicting the Greek goddess of war and wisdom, Athena, with her name inscribed in Greek letters written in reverse, indicating that the ring was used as a seal. She was also wearing elaborate pendants of gold with turquoise, garnet, lapis lazuli, carnelian, and pearls, which depicted a man (dubbed the "Dragon Master") in typical nomadic clothing grasping two dragons. Other important treasures from the burial mound included a silver Chinese mirror, an Indian ivory comb, a magnificent intricately worked gold and turquoise boot buckle, gold and turquoise belt buckles depicting a boy on a dolphin, a detailed gold figure of a winged Aphrodite with an Indian bindi (ornamental dot) between her eyebrows, an iron dagger with a gold and turquoise handle depicting animals and a dancing bear, and a gold coin of the Roman emperor, Tiberius, minted 3,000 miles away in Lyon, southern France, between AD 14 and AD 37. This latter coin is the first of its kind to be found in all of Central Asia.

After examining the vast collection of about 20,600 gold ornaments retrieved from the necropolis at Tillya Tepe, the archaeologists realized that they represented an extraordinary range of influences from China, Siberia, Persia, India, Rome, and Greece, and also reflected the wide sphere of nomad migration and contacts. American archaeologist Fredrik Hiebert, of the National Geographic Society, has noted how the nomads of Tillya Tepe had taken the iconography from these far-flung cultures and blended it together into their own unique style of art.

In the winter of 1978–1979, while the archaeologists were carefully photographing and recording every last piece of the treasure from Tillya Tepe, they became aware that news of the value of their discovery had leaked out. Soon the Afghan army had to be called in to guard the site from looters and armed tribesmen. In February 1979, Sarianidi decided to abandon the site, before he had the chance to excavate a newly discovered seventh grave (this was later robbed by looters) and took the treasure to the National Museum in Kabul. On December 24, 1979, Soviet troops entered Afghanistan, leading the country into 23 years of war and chaos, which would leave 1.7 million people dead.

In 1989, after the Soviet withdrawal from the country, President Najibullah's government and National Museum officials planned to transfer many of the objects from the Kabul Museum to secret hiding places for safety. But nothing more was heard of this plan, and no one seemed to know if it had been carried out.

In the absence of news of the Bactrian Gold it was speculated that during the years of turmoil in Afghanistan the artifacts had either been melted down to buy arms, sold on the black market, or stolen and taken to Moscow by Soviet troops. Following the departure of the Soviets, years of civil war reduced parts of Kabul to ruins, and the museum suffered terribly at the hands of looters and vandals, with thousands of irreplaceable artifacts destroyed or missing. In 1994, while the museum was being used as a military base, it was shelled, its roof and top floor destroyed.

Researchers wondered how the Bactrian Gold could have survived such chaos. When the Taliban took Kabul in 1996, Najibullah, by then in hiding after the collapse of his government, was tortured and murdered. The Taliban then turned their attention to Da Afghanistan Bank (the country's Central Bank). They forced employees to open the vault used for keeping national treasure and went inside to check that the country's gold reserves were intact. Satisfied that everything was in order, they left. However, the Taliban later began a systematic destruction of non-Islamic art and, in February 2001, ordered that all idols, including the two monumental Buddhas of Bamiyan Valley, central Afghanistan, were to be destroyed. The Buddhas were dynamited in March of that year, and many thousands more irreplaceable artifacts throughout the country were lost.

In November 2001, during the U.S. invasion of Afghanistan, the Taliban made a desperate attempt to get at the gold bullion from the vault inside the Central Bank; although they managed to steal millions of dollars in cash, they were unable to break in to the vault. Eventually they were forced to flee in the face of approaching Northern Alliance and American forces.

On August 28, 2003, Afghanistan's new government arranged to have the vault opened, and after doing so informed the world that everything was safe (in all, $90m in gold bars and coins and another $20m in cash). There was no mention of the Bactrian Gold. But it was there, hidden in six ordinary museum trunks, buried under crates of old coins, exactly where it had been placed by museum staff in 1989, along with a total of 200 crates of ancient artifacts from the National Museum. How had such a priceless treasure been missed by the Taliban? The story that emerged was both heroic and inspiring, and not a little reminiscent of a Dan Brown novel or an Indiana Jones movie.

When the hoard had been moved from the museum to the Central Bank at the Presidential Palace in 1989, the doors of the underground vault were locked with keys that were given to five trustworthy museum guards and curators. The treasure was under the supervision of Omara Khan Masoudi, the museum's director, and one of the five "key holders," and the vault door could only be opened if all the keys were used. Each of the key holders (called "tawadars") was sworn to secrecy and put their lives at risk in not revealing the location of the keys or the treasure, or handing the keys over to the Taliban. If any of the key holders died, they were to pass the keys on to their eldest sons. When the Taliban came to check on the vault in 1996, it was the job of one of the key holders, known as "Mr. Mustafa" (to protect his identity), to lock the steel door behind them when they left. Taking his life in his hands Mr. Mustafa decided that the Taliban must be prevented from getting their hands on Afghanistan's ancient treasures, so he turned the key backward in the lock, snapping it in two and leaving a fragment jammed inside. Mr. Mustafa told no one what he had done. When the Taliban returned to the vault in 2001 and attempted to open the door again, they were unable to see the fragment of broken metal inside the lock from Mr. Mustafa's key. Thus they went away empty-handed. If this had been discovered it would certainly have meant instant execution.

Before Hamid Karzai's Afghan government could open the vault in 2003, it was faced with a problem: One of the key holders had disappeared a number of years before. For a while the government considered breaking open the vault, but eventually decided to appoint a judge from the Ministry of Justice as a substitute key holder. After the crates were opened in March 2004, their contents had to be authenticated and catalogued. For this purpose a team of local and international experts, which included archaeologist Fredrik Hiebert, was assembled. In 2004 it was announced to the world that the Bactrian Gold had been recovered completely intact; indeed the artifacts were found still wrapped in the same tissue paper in which the museum staff had put them 15 years earlier.

Later that year there came another astonishing episode in the drama of Afghanistan's ancient past when it was announced that some of the Begram Ivories, stolen in 1992 from the National Museum in Kabul at the height of the Afghan civil war, had been recovered. The Begram Ivories are a priceless series of 2,000-year-old intricately carved and colored Indian ivory inlays excavated in the 1930s from ancient Begram, a trading city on the Silk Road about 80 miles north of Kabul. More than a thousand of these ivories were found by French archaeologists as part of a spectacular hoard that also contained bronzes and glassware from Roman Egypt and Syria, and lacquered bowls from China. Since the Soviet withdrawal from Afghanistan, the pieces from the Begram Ivories had been sitting in the same vault inside the Central Bank as the Bactrian Gold. In 2010, further ivories from the Hoard, which had been sold on the black market to buyers abroad, were recovered and sent back to the National Museum at Kabul.

Since 2004 selections from the Bactrian Gold and other pieces from Afghanistan's ancient treasures have been displayed at some of the world's finest museums. The incredibly successful exhibition *Afghanistan: Hidden Treasures From the National Museum, Kabul* traveled first to the Guimet Museum in Paris in December 2006, then to the Museo di Antichità in Turin, Italy, and the Nieuwe Kerk in Amsterdam. In 2008–2009 the exhibition visited the United States and Canada, traveling to the National Gallery of Art in Washington, DC; the Metropolitan Museum of Art in New York City; the Asian Art Museum of San Francisco; the Museum of Fine Arts in Houston, Texas; and the Canadian Museum of Civilization Gatineau in Quebec. In 2010 the exhibition reached the Bonn Museum in Germany and in 2011 the British Museum in London.

In recent years the National Museum in Kabul has been rebuilt with the aid of UNESCO and various international donors, who gave in excess of $350,000 to the project. It is hoped that one day the Bactrian Gold will be displayed either in the renovated museum or a new building built in Kabul especially for the purpose. Organizers of *Afghanistan: Hidden Treasures From the National Museum, Kabul* have described the story of the Bactrian Gold as "a triumph of culture and beauty over vandalism and bigotry."[1] Indeed it is a not only a story with a happy ending, but is also a symbol of hope for the future of Afghanistan, a country with a rich archaeological heritage, testament to its position at the crossroads for trade on the ancient Silk Road.

*The Staffordshire Hoard*

In July 2009 a local metal detectorist scanning a field in Staffordshire in the English Midlands came upon a large group of metal objects. What he was about to uncover was to change English history. The collection of about 1,500 late-sixth- to eighth-century gold and silver objects is the biggest Anglo-Saxon hoard of metalwork ever discovered anywhere in the world. Moreover, much of the metalwork is decorated with precious stones, some of which came from as far away as India or possibly even Sri Lanka. Parallels were immediately drawn with the magnificent objects from the world-famous Sutton Hoo ship burial, the seventh-century grave of a king buried in his wooden ship, discovered in East Anglia in 1939.

What is most surprising is that the vast majority of the items in the Staffordshire Hoard are weapon parts and martial items; there are no domestic or feminine pieces at all. It has been speculated that the treasure is a collection of war trophies stripped from defeated enemies, but if so, who looted the items and why did they bury them together afterward? Was it pagans or Christians? The treasure points to a battle or battles fought by one of the kings of Mercia (an Anglo-Saxon kingdom of central England) but whether this was Penda (the last pagan king of Mercia), Wulfhere, or Æthelred, or, more interestingly, a previously unrecorded monarch of the area, only future research will tell.

On the morning of July 5, 2009, Terry Herbert, a 55-year-old former coffin maker from Burntwood, was searching a recently plowed field in Hammerwich, near Lichfield in Staffordshire using his 14-year-old metal detector. Just before noon Herbert's machine indicated something interesting below the soil and he began to dig down with a spade, eventually unearthing a piece of what he first thought was brass. On closer examination, however, he realized it may be gold and excitedly carried on digging until he had discovered several more pieces. Throughout the next five days, Mr. Herbert, who lived alone in a council flat on disability benefit, had filled 244 bags with the extraordinary finds and decided he needed help. As he was obliged to do under the 1996 Treasure Act, Herbert contacted Duncan Slarke, the Finds Liaison Officer for the Staffordshire and West Midlands Portable Antiquities Scheme, who is based at Birmingham Museums and Art Gallery (BMAG). An arrangement was then made with landowner Fred Johnson for an archaeological excavation to search for any remaining pieces from the hoard. All this had to be done in extreme secrecy to protect the site from so called "nighthawkers" (thieves with metal detectors who remove objects at night from protected sites), which was a difficult undertaking, as the location of the hoard was close to major roads and thus was extremely exposed to the public.

The excavation of the field, funded by English Heritage and Staffordshire County Council, was undertaken between July 24, 2009, and August 21, 2009, by Birmingham Archaeology. By the end of the excavations the Staffordshire Hoard numbered 3,940 separate fragments and objects including silver, gold, and garnet-inlaid sword hilts, pommels, sword pyramids (toggles that may have been used to suspend scabbards belts), helmet fragments, and gold Christian crosses, all of extraordinary craftsmanship. There is so much material in the hoard that it doubles the amount of

Anglo-Saxon metalwork so far discovered in England. In weight the hoard totals 11.2 pounds of gold, 3.2 pounds of silver, and includes an astonishing 3,500 cloisonné garnets. (Cloisonné is a style of enamel decoration where the enamel is applied and fired in raised cells on a metal background.) The outstanding items in the collection include a gold pectoral cross decorated with a circular filigree pattern with a red garnet in its center (such an item would have been worn by senior clergy or by wealthy Christian laypeople); an exquisitely adorned silver helmet cheek piece decorated with four bands of running, interlaced animals; a gold sword pyramid decorated with cloisonné garnets and blue glass; a gold sword hilt plate with zoomorphic decoration; a gold stylized horse or seahorse with exquisite filigree decoration; and a silver gilt strip inscribed with a verse from the Latin Bible *"Surge domine et dissipentur inimici tui et fugiant qui oderunt te a facie tua"* ("Rise up, o Lord, and may thy enemies be scattered and those who hate thee be driven from thy face").

*11.1. Hilt fitting from the Staffordshire Hoard. Photo by Daniel Buxton, Birmingham Museum and Art Gallery. Licensed under the Creative Commons Attribution 2.0 Generic license on Wikipedia.*

The vast majority of the objects from the hoard are damaged in some way (either bent, twisted, scratched, or broken); although a small amount of this can be attributed to plow damage, most seems to have occurred before the items were deposited. Experts have theorized that this damage may have happened when the fittings were removed from their original settings (like the gold hilt plate, for example), and when objects were folded or compacted (as was one of the Christian gold crosses) to fit into the chest or vessel that probably once contained the hoard.

Because there has been no similar find in terms of size and quality, drawing comparisons with the Staffordshire Hoard has been difficult. The closest parallel to the hoard comes from the site of Sutton Hoo, near Woodbridge, in Suffolk, in the east of England, which was first excavated just before the outbreak of WWII. The burial from Mound 1 at Sutton Hoo (one of many burials at the site) is thought to be of the seventh-century Anglo-Saxon King Raedwald, who died around AD 624, and was discovered under a large mound that contained a 90-foot-long wooden ship. The grave produced a stunning collection of finds, including gold and garnet weapon fittings, gold coins, silver vessels and silver-mounted drinking horns and cups, an iron sword with a gold and garnet pommel, and a magnificently decorated paneled helmet. The burial also contained domestic items such as bronze cauldrons, an iron-bound tub, and a bucket. There are certainly close similarities between the types of artifacts from the Staffordshire Hoard and those from Sutton Hoo, including the sheer quality of the craftsmanship evident in the items, their design, and the presence of a rare Anglo-Saxon helmet (though only fragments in the case of the Staffordshire Hoard). However, there are also many differences, such as the presence of coins and domestic items at Sutton Hoo. Unfortunately as the contexts of the two finds are so different, comparisons between them can only tell us a limited amount about the Staffordshire Hoard.

Though nothing securely datable has been identified so far from the Staffordshire Hoard, help with dating has been provided by comparisons with the objects from the Sutton Hoo burial, which can give a rough date range mainly because of the coins found alongside them. Anglo-Saxon specialists believe the items in the Staffordshire collection range in date from the late sixth century AD to the beginning of the eighth century AD, and were originally buried in a wooden or leather container, within a pit. Something that became apparent to scholars of Anglo-Saxon England as soon as the finds from the hoard had been categorized was what was missing from a typical hoard of the period: There are no domestic items, such as vessels or eating utensils in the hoard, and no objects that can be associated with women, such as dress pins, brooches, and pendants; there are also no sword or knife blades, no recognizable harness fittings, no coins, no Anglo-Saxon iron, and the large masculine gold buckles commonly found in male Anglo-Saxon burials such as Sutton Hoo are completely absent.

Furthermore, although the find spot of the hoard is next to the Roman Watling Street (modern A5) and just a couple of miles from the Roman town of Letocetum, not a single find from the Roman period was recovered by Terry Herbert or by archaeologists during the excavations. Another surprising feature of the Staffordshire Hoard is that it is largely made up of military items, primarily high-quality fittings that have been removed from the hilts of swords and daggers. Dr. Kevin Leahy, former curator at North Lincolnshire Museum, has theorized that the gold fittings may have been removed to depersonalize the objects, removing the identity of the previous owners; the iron blades of the weapons may have then been reused. Another point noticed by experts is that some objects in the hoard are unique in terms of Anglo-Saxon artifacts and have no known parallels. The conclusion can only be that the items in this incomparable collection were carefully chosen, but for what purpose remains a mystery, though the possibility remains that the hoard was only part of a larger assemblage of artifacts, the rest of which is yet to be discovered.

*11.2. A selection of pieces from the Staffordshire Hoard. Photo by David Rowan, Birmingham Museum and Art Gallery. Licensed under the Creative Commons Attribution 2.0 Generic license on Wikipedia.*

What of the origins of the items in the hoard? Were they made on the continent, locally in Mercia, or in another kingdom of Anglo-Saxon England? And where did the raw material come from? The Staffordshire Hoard Conservation Project, an integrated research and conservation program based at BMAG, has been researching the items in the hoard, but it is still early days. Unfortunately, it is unlikely that the origins of the gold used to manufacture so many of the objects in the hoard will ever be traced. Gold is such a valuable material that it is constantly being melted down, and afterward is frequently mixed with other gold and fashioned into new objects. Once this has happened it is not possible to say where any of the gold originally came from.

If the gold objects in the Staffordshire Hoard were created from melted-down objects, one intriguing possibility, put forward by Dr. David Symons, curator of antiquities at BMAG, is that the gold may have been sourced from the rich Byzantine Empire; gold Byzantine coins have been suggested as one possibility. In

July 2011 Graeme McArthur at BMAG analyzed two gold items from the hoard using X-ray fluorescence and discovered that they contained 94 percent gold (around 22 carats), much higher than the majority of modern gold. In November 2011, a number of items from the hoard were sent to the Louvre in Paris for scientific analysis. The garnets from the collection were subjected to particle-induced X-ray emission, Raman spectroscopy, and X-ray fluorescence at the EU-funded CHARISMA project. The results were interesting, to say the least. The chemical composition of the gemstones indicated that the majority of the small deep red examples came from Bohemia (a historical region occupying the western part of the Czech Republic), whereas others originated in eastern India or Sri Lanka. The fascinating conclusion from these tests is that the garnets would probably have arrived in England through Roman trade networks.

The questions of who deposited the hoard, when, and why are still in the process of investigation. But there are a few theories worth mentioning. One theory, that the objects were deposited as a bullion hoard, can be discounted, as one would expect at least a small amount of gold coins in such a collection, but there is not a single coin in the cache. Furthermore, why would a bullion hoard be restricted to military items?

The Staffordshire Hoard was discovered at the heart of the Anglo-Saxon kingdom of Mercia, by AD 600, one of the seven principal Anglo-Saxon kingdoms of England (sometimes referred to as the Heptarchy), the others being Wessex, Northumbria, East Anglia, Kent, Sussex, and Essex. The seventh century in England was a violent and turbulent time, with battles between native Britons and Anglo-Saxons (who had settled in Britain from the mid-fifth century AD), as well as between pagan and Christian armies. Contemporary written sources for the kingdom of Mercia are scant; the main source for early Anglo-Saxon England as a whole is Bede's *Historia ecclesiastica gentis Anglorum* (*Ecclesiastical History of the English People*), completed around AD 731, and the first work of history in which the AD system of dating was used. Bede was a priest at the Monastery of Saint Paul's in Jarrow in

Northumberland (a kingdom in modern northeast England and southeast Scotland), so naturally his history is written from a Christian perspective and focuses mainly on the church. Bearing in mind his religious bias, Bede may not have had much interest in a kingdom like Mercia, which was essentially pagan until the second half part of the seventh century.

Historian, author, and TV presenter Michael Wood has suggested that the Staffordshire Hoard could have been a ransom paid to the Mercian pagan king Penda (died AD 655). Wood believes that the treasure may have formed part of a payment made to Penda by the Northumbrian king Oswiu (c AD 612–670) after Penda's Mercian army had besieged Oswiu at the Battle of Winwaed (probably in modern Yorkshire) in AD 655. According to Bede, Oswiu had tried to buy off the Mercian king with "an incalculable quantity of regalia and presents as the price of peace."[1] However, Bede also notes that Penda refused the bribe, which would suggest that these items did not find their way south to Mercia to become the Staffordshire Hoard. Penda was also slain in the battle, which would seem to preclude any chance of the treasure falling into Mercian hands.

According to the ninth-century poem "Marwnad Cynddylan" ("The Death-song of Cynddylan"), around AD 636, Morfael, a British leader from Powys (in modern mid-Wales), attacked a place called "Caer Lwytgoed" ("the fortification in the gray wood"), took all the movable wealth of the city, and killed a bishop and a number of monks. The site of Caer Lwytgoed has been much debated but the previously mentioned Roman settlement of Letocetum has been put forward as a candidate, though there is no evidence that it was inhabited later than the fifth century AD. An alternative is the neighboring cathedral city of Lichfield, a place-name interpreted by some researchers as meaning "the field of corpses" and thus a possible site of the mysterious battle. However, the name "Lichfield" is more correctly understood to mean "common pasture in (or beside) gray wood," and recorded history does not begin at Lichfield until St. Chad arrived to establish his Bishopric in AD 669, though that does not mean, of course, that it was not inhabited before this date. Perhaps the site of Caer Lwytgoed is yet to be found in this area.

Another important battle involving the Mercians took place in AD 679, when King Ecgfrith (reigned AD 670–685) brought his Northumbrian army into Mercian territory only to be defeated by King Æthelred at the Battle of the Trent. (The River Trent flows north from Biddulph Moor in Staffordshire.) Could the Staffordshire Hoard represent an enormous ritual deposit, dedicated to pagan gods in thanks for this victory? Though the wide date range of the items in the hoard would preclude them originating as the spoils from a single battle, they may have been captured over a long series of military campaigns by a Mercian king, perhaps Penda (reigned AD 626–655), Wulfhere (reigned AD 658–675), or Æthelred (reigned AD 675–704). Another theory is that the hoard could have been a tribute payment made to Mercia by another Anglo-Saxon kingdom; if a certain weight in silver and gold was demanded, then this might explain the selection of items in the collection. Alternatively, the hoard may represent a royal treasury, such as that possessed by Northumbrian King Edwin (died AD 632/633), which, according to Bede, included a large gold cross, and a golden chalice. Perhaps the Mercian royal treasury was secreted in a field beside Watling Street in a period when Mercia was threatened from outside—after King Penda was defeated at Winwaed in AD 655, for instance. But although the extremely high quality of the craftsmanship and the material of the hoard may support this theory, the absence of whole weapons and the inclusion of almost-exclusively military items would suggest otherwise.

Beyond the fact that the hoard was deposited hurriedly in an isolated spot in an area without known Anglo-Saxon buildings, suggesting someone on the run who, for whatever reason, was never able to come back and retrieve the treasure, little else can be said at the moment with any degree of certainty. In the end, because the hoard was only discovered in 2009 and there is such a huge amount of material, a lot more work needs to be done before we are even sure of the dating of the items, never mind their origins and meaning.

The discovery of the Staffordshire Hoard was publicly announced on September 24, 2009, and attracted worldwide attention. The hoard was declared to be treasure at a coroner's inquest held on September 24, 2009, and under the 1996 Treasure Act the finder and landowner were eligible to be rewarded for the full market value of the find, to be shared equally between them. On November 25, 2009, the hoard was valued by the Treasure Valuation Committee at £3.285 million ($5.306 million), and shortly afterward it was announced that the BMAG and the Potteries Museum & Art Gallery, Stoke-on-Trent, Staffordshire, were to jointly purchase the complete hoard. The Art Fund then launched a public appeal to raise the necessary funds with a deadline of April 17, 2010. If the money was not raised by this time the hoard could have been sold on the open market, and the unparalleled collection permanently broken up and scattered throughout the world. Thankfully, the necessary funds were raised ahead of time and the Staffordshire Hoard remained in the English Midlands, where it was originally discovered.

As the finds were still being processed, some pieces from the hoard were put on display at the BMAG until October 13, 2009, and a further selection of items from the hoard was displayed at the Potteries Museum & Art Gallery. Further displays of artifacts from the hoard took place at the British Museum (from November 3, 2009, until April 17, 2010) and at the National Geographic Museum in Washington, DC (from October 29, 2011, to March 4, 2012). A number of items from the Staffordshire Hoard are currently on display in Gallery 16 of the BMAG, and many are still in the process of being examined and conserved. Already the Staffordshire Hoard has opened an astonishing window onto the world of the Anglo-Saxons, further cleaning and examination of the exquisite and sometimes mysterious objects can only shed more light on trade, religious practices, crafts, technology, and warfare in what for too long have been known as England's Dark Ages.

# Viking Hoards

The Vikings are renowned for their violent raids and invasions, from the Caspian Sea in the east to North America in the west, but they were also voyagers, colonizers, and traders. They left behind a fascinating legacy of these activities in the form of a number of treasure hoards, buried in the ground for religious or political reasons, or often simply for safekeeping. Some of the richest and best known of these Viking hoard come from England, including the Cuerdale Hoard of 8,600 items, including silver coins, jewelry, and silver ingots; and the Harrogate/Vale of York Hoard of 617 silver coins and 65 ornaments, ingots, and pieces of precious metal, found hidden in a gilt silver vessel lined with gold. There are also rich Viking hoards from the island of Gotland in the Viking homeland of Sweden, and from Russia. Viking warriors, merchants, and rulers seem to have buried a substantial part of their wealth in these hoards and the fascinating objects found within can tell us a significant amount about the Viking economy, their trade routes and practices, and the spread of Christianity in Viking areas.

12.1. *Silver pennies from the Vale of York hoard. Image by JMaill. Licensed under the Creative Commons Attribution-Share Alike 3.0 Unported license on Wikipedia.*

During the Viking Age (late eighth to 11th centuries) there was an extremely high rate of deposition of metal and metal objects in the ground throughout Britain, Ireland, Northern and Eastern Europe, and Russia. These hoards have been discovered in practically every area the Vikings occupied and contain mostly silver objects such as coins, ingots, personal ornaments, and fragments of metal known as hack-silver. Hack-silver was made when large ornaments or pieces of jewelry were chopped up into small fragments in order to make bullion of certain weights, thus facilitating exchange using these exact weights. Small, portable scales capable of accurate weighing have been found in excavations of Viking sites, showing that a controlled system of trade and exchange was in operation even without the use of regular coinage. Coins and coin fragments, which the Vikings obtained through trade and trading contacts in Europe and the Islamic world, were valued for their weight in silver or gold and the purity of the metal, rather than having any intrinsic monetary value. Metallurgical studies have shown that a high proportion of the Islamic coins that found their way to Scandinavia at this time were cut up for use as hack-silver or sometimes melted down for reuse as jewelry or silver ingots. Indeed, the vast majority of Viking silver objects found in southern Sweden were made from melted-down *dirhams* (silver coins) of the Samanid Dynasty (AD 819–999) of Central Asia and Greater Iran. Silver was by far the most common metal used in the Viking economy and was circulated in the form of bars, ingots, jewelry, and hack-silver. With no local sources of the precious metal, the Vikings were forced to engage in trade or plunder to obtain it.

The coins from Viking hoards can give us valuable information in terms of the areas where they were minted. Mints identified from Viking hoards include Dublin (Ireland), Quentovic (possibly modern Étaples in northern France), Aquitaine (France), Touraine (France), Ribe or Hedeby (Denmark), Lund (Denmark), London (UK), and York (UK), as well as various Byzantine and Islamic mints. Such a wide variety of coin mints illustrate the extent of Viking trade contacts.

The treasures contained in Viking hoards could be amassed from plunder, trade, tributes, fines, or bride wealth (payment made by a groom or his family to the kin of the bride upon her marriage to the groom). There must have been a wide variety of reasons why the Vikings deposited these hoards in the ground, depending on the person and the circumstances involved. The most basic reason would be that a person secreted away family or individual wealth during periods of turmoil and was never able to recover it because he or she was killed, captured, or forced to leave his or her property. This scenario may be linked to a display of wealth by political leaders, who would have kept caches of silver to dole out to their followers in order to reinforce their political influence. Another possibility is that the wealth was deposited in peaceful times as a primitive form of banking, insuring the person against future financial difficulties, and for whatever reason was never recovered. A further suggestion is that wealth would be deposited underground just before a person embarked on a potentially dangerous voyage.

Religious reasons are another possibility, when the buried cache perhaps formed part of a pagan ritual offering—possibly the grave goods of a warrior on his way to Valhalla. Any artifacts buried with the warrior were believed to accompany the dead man to the afterlife. There is some suggestion of this ritual connection in the Old English heroic epic *Beowulf,* dated between the eighth and the early-11th centuries. In the final act of the poem, set in the early sixth century AD in Scandinavia, Beowulf and his companion, Wiglaf, slay a dragon and take its treasure hoard. But the hero is fatally wounded by the dragon in the fight and dies soon afterward. Beowulf is cremated and entombed in a burial mound along with funeral goods and the Dragon's hoard. The treasure is buried with the hero in order to ritually return it to the earth where it belongs or perhaps because it is cursed.

Another version of ritual hoarding has been suggested where the act of burying wealth removes items from circulation that are usually expected to be distributed in Viking society. This act could also be related to the display of wealth and power mentioned earlier, where a grandiose destruction of wealth graphically illustrates the power and affluence of the individual. In the Icelandic epic *Egils saga,* the oldest transcript of which dates back to AD 1240, the hero, Egil Skallagrimsson, sinks his silver treasure in a bog with a stone slab the day before he dies. To ensure the location of the cache is kept secret, Egil then kills the two servants who helped him put it there.

One of the largest and most important of all Viking hoards is that from Cuerdale, near Preston, Lancashire, in the northwest of England. On May 15, 1840, workmen repairing an embankment on the southern side of the River Ribble discovered the remains of a lead-lined chest containing 8,600 items of silver coins and bullion weighing almost 90 pounds. The workmen tried to pocket some of the silver coins, but when the bailiff arrived were ordered to put them back, though they were allowed to keep one coin each from the hoard. It is likely, however, that many coins from the original hoard were stolen before the bailiff arrived. In August 1840 the hoard was dispersed to more than 170 recipients, though the majority was given to the British Museum. Other pieces from the Cuerdale Hoard eventually found their way to the National Museums Liverpool and the Ashmolean Museum (Oxford).

The astonishing collection of Viking treasure in the Cuerdale Hoard included silver coins, armlets, chains, rings, amulets, hack-silver, and ingots of various shapes and weights. Five small bone pins were also discovered with the cache (though they have since disappeared), indicating that some of the objects had been contained in separate cloth bags or parcels, held together by these pins. The silver bullion made up the majority of the hoard, weighing more than 80 pounds. The hack silver consisted of cut up arm rings and brooches of Norse, Pictish (from eastern and northern Scotland), Irish, and Carolingian (French) origin. The diverse nature of the hack-silver illustrates the wide-ranging nature of Viking trade, contact, and raiding. The international reach of the Vikings is also borne out by the origins of a number of the 7,000 coins from the Cuerdale Hoard. Experts have divided the coins into three categories, according to their source. So we have 5,000 coins from the Viking kingdoms of eastern England, minted at York around AD 900; 1,000 Anglo-Saxon issues of the ninth and 10th centuries; and coins of foreign origin. The oldest of the Anglo-Saxon coins in the hoard is a beautiful and unique penny of Ceolwulf II of Mercia (died c AD 881), which was probably minted in the 870s.

The foreign coins from the Cuerdale Hoard provide a fascinating insight into Viking trade networks. The oldest coin in the entire hoard is a Byzantine silver hexagram of Heraclius and Heraclius Constantine, minted between AD 615 and 630. There are also early Scandinavian, Carolingian, North Italian, and papal coins, as well as around 50 Kufic dirhams from the Islamic world. The Carolingian coins were the result of repeated Viking raids on the country, whereas most of the other foreign coinage came to Britain via Scandinavia. The most recent coin in the collection was minted in AD 905 by Louis the Blind (AD 880–928), emperor of the West Franks (who ruled an area roughly equivalent to modern-day France). Being the latest coin in the collection, this gives a fairly accurate terminal date for the deposition of the treasure.

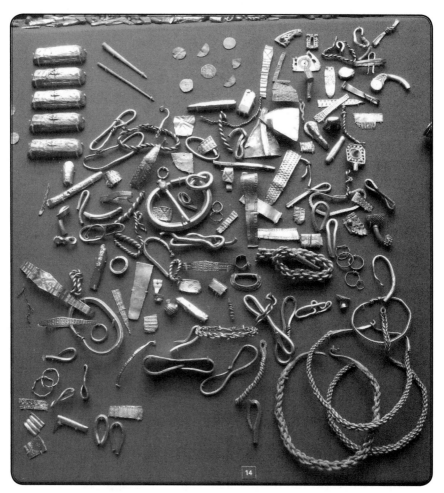

*12.2. Some of the Viking silver from the Cuerdale Hoard in the British Museum. Image by JMaill. Licensed under the Creative Commons Attribution-Share Alike 3.0 Unported license on Wikipedia.*

Furthermore, the local Viking coins from the hoard were fairly new, suggesting that the treasure was buried only two or three years after the coinage was first introduced. Thus the coins would suggest that the hoard must have been buried between 905 and 910. This date is only a few years after the Vikings were expelled from Dublin (in 902) and, taken together with the Irish origin of a large amount of the silver jewelry, would suggest that the hoard is perhaps a war chest, assembled by Vikings exiles from Ireland. Perhaps these exiles planned a military assault to reoccupy Dublin from a base on the River Ribble, and Cuerdale does lie on an overland route from Viking York to the Irish Sea. But this plan apparently didn't work out, and the Vikings never returned to Cuerdale to recover their extraordinary rich treasure.

Another remarkable English Viking hoard comes from near the town of Harrogate in North Yorkshire. Known as the Vale of York Hoard or the Harrogate Hoard, this cache of 617 silver coins and 65 other items, including ornaments, ingots, and hack-silver, was discovered inside the remains of a lead chest in an empty field on January 6, 2007, by metal detectorist David Whelan and his son Andrew. After discovering the Viking treasure, the largest discovered in Britain since the Cuerdale Hoard, Whelan followed the law and reported the find to Amy Cooper, Finds Liaison Officer of the Portable Antiquities Scheme. The Whelans also had the foresight not only to collect every scrap of material from the find spot but also to record the precise location of the hoard, enabling archaeologists to examine the exact site of the deposition in detail, though no further evidence of Viking activity was found. One wishes all treasure hunters were this conscientious.

The most impressive objects in the Harrogate Hoard are a rare gold arm-ring (possibly of Irish origin), a fragment of a twisted silver neck-ring from northern Russia, and an exquisite mid-ninth-century gilt silver cup or bowl (originating from what is now France or western Germany), decorated with vine leaf scrolls and hunting scenes showing lions, stags, and a horse. Most of the smaller items had been put inside this silver bowl before this was placed inside the lead chest; consequently the objects from the hoard were extremely well-preserved. Experts believe that the silver vessel was used to hold communion bread and was either looted from a church or monastery in the northern Frankish Empire or given in tribute. The 617 coins in the hoard, which, like those from the Cuerdale Hoard, are a mixture of Anglo-Saxon, Anglo-Scandinavian, Islamic, and Carolingian, date from the late ninth and early 10th centuries, thus giving a date for the deposition of the Harrogate Hoard in the early 10th century, probably around AD 928. The coins from the hoard shine a fascinating light on the extensive contacts of the Vikings and their cultural and religious diversity, bearing Islamic, Christian, and pre-Christian Norse pagan symbols; some even mixed Christian and pagan imagery, giving important insights into the newly Christianized Vikings and their beliefs. A good illustration of this Christianization comes in the form of a number of coins from the hoard that were minted in Viking York and stamped with a dedication to St. Peter and a Viking stylized hammer, symbol of the Viking god Thor.

Other coins in the hoard give us important political information on northern England during the ninth and 10th centuries. One of the Viking silver pennies from the hoard was issued at a previously unrecorded mint of RORIVACASTR, thought to be modern-day Rocester, to the north of Uttoxeter, Staffordshire This coin is not only important because it came from an unknown mint, but because it suggests something that historians were not aware of: that Viking control during this period extended into the English Midlands. Most of the English silver pennies from the hoard date from AD 880 onward (the latter part of King Alfred's reign and the early part of the reign of his son Edward the Elder). Motifs and buildings stamped on some rare examples of these coins show that Edward and his sister Æthelflæd (ruler of the Anglo-Saxon kingdom of Mercia from AD 911–918) extended their authority in the Midlands at this time. The latest coins in the hoard belong to the reign of Anglo-Saxon King Athelstan (AD 924–939), who conquered Viking Northumbria (northern England and southeast Scotland) in 927, an important moment in the unification of England. The latest coin from the treasure (introduced in 927/928) celebrates this accomplishment and gives Athelstan the title of "REX TOTIUS BRITANNIAE" ("King of all Britain").

The Harrogate Hoard may well be related to the Anglo-Saxon victory in Northumbria, perhaps belonging to a wealthy Viking leader who buried it for safekeeping during the unrest that followed the conquest. With objects originating from places as far apart as Ireland in the west and Russia and Afghanistan in the east, the Harrogate Hoard illustrates the wide extent of Viking travels and trade links, and the diversity of their cultural contacts in the first quarter of the 10th century. In July 2007, the Hoard was transferred to the British Museum and later valued by the independent Treasure Valuation Committee at £1.08 million ($1.75 million). The treasure was purchased jointly by the York Museums Trust and the British Museum with help from funding from the National Heritage Memorial Fund, the Art Fund, and the British Museum Friends. The money from the Harrogate Hoard was split between the finders (the Whelans) and the landowners, showing that when hunting for treasure doing the right thing can sometimes bring rich rewards.

Before we leave Viking England, one more treasure hoard is worthy of a brief mention. This is the Silverdale Hoard, discovered by metal detectorists in September 2011, in a field just outside the village of Silverdale, near the coast in north Lancashire (northwest England), only around 60 miles from where the Cuerdale Hoard was found. This huge collection of more than 200 pieces of silver jewelry was found inside a lead container and included 10 complete arm rings, two finger rings, brooch fragments, a fine wire braid, and 141 pieces of hack-silver. The finds date to around AD 905–910, a little earlier than the Harrogate Hoard but also during the same period of bitter struggles between the Vikings and the Anglo-Saxons in the north of England. The most interesting find from the Hoard is what has become known as the Airdeconut coin. This unique coin is stamped with the name "Airdeconut" (probably an Anglo-Saxon rendition of the Viking "Harthacnut"), a previously unknown Viking ruler of northern England. The reverse of the coin bears a Christian inscription "DNS (Dominus) REX" with the letters arranged in the form of a cross. The coin, dated to around AD 900, illustrates that only a few decades after the Vikings began permanent settlement in Britain they had converted to Christianity.

Viking presence in Russia dates from as far back as AD 750. Indeed the name Russia is believed by some scholars to originate from Vikings known as "Rus' people" who came to modern Estonia, Ukraine, and Russia through the trade routes from Sweden. There are numerous Viking hoards from the area of modern Russia, including those from the medieval cities of Novgorod, St. Petersburg, and Staraya Ladoga, testament to close trading links with the Viking homeland. On May 17, 1988, a Viking silver hoard was apparently discovered near the Spasskiye Gates in the Kremlin in Moscow, a site that has been continuously inhabited since the second century BC. Although there is little information available about this find, the hoard included 10 hollow pendants and an arm ring made from several strands of silver with gilded dragon heads at its ends. This arm ring is thought to have originated in the island of Gotland, in the Baltic Sea, east of the Swedish mainland, right in the heart of the Viking homeland.

Between 700 and 800 Viking silver hoards have been reported on Gotland, which makes a lot of sense when one considers the geographical location of the island, in the middle of the trade routes between Western and Eastern Europe. There are no natural sources of silver on Gotland, so the treasure hoards found on the island must be a result of Viking raids, political alliances, marriages, tributes, and trading contacts with Europe and the Middle East.

A huge Viking hoard was discovered in 1999 at Spillings Farm, near the Bay of Boge, in the north of Gotland. This vast treasure included 14,295 silver coins, 486 silver armlets, and bronze objects from the eastern Baltic. The latest date for the hoard, given by the coins in the collection, is AD 870/1. In 2000, Swedish archaeologists excavating a Viking site near a harbor on Gotland discovered one of the largest Viking hoards to date. The treasure consisted of 13,000 Arabic silver coins, 500 arm bands and bracelets, numerous silver bars, rings, and hack-silver, valued today at £400,000 ($646,140). The hoard had been buried around the same time as the Spillings Hoard, c AD 870, under the floorboards of a wealthy merchant's house, presumably for safekeeping. Other notable hoards from Gotland include two from Ocksarve in Hemse parish, in the south of the island. The first of these hoards was discovered in 1920, the second in 1997. The first hoard is remarkable for the 123 Byzantine silver coins it contained (only around 400 Byzantine silver coins have ever been found in Scandinavia), the vast majority of which belonged to Emperor Constantine IX Monomachos (AD 1042–1055). Experts believe these Byzantine coins may have been part of the salary of a Viking mercenary, perhaps a former member of the Varangian guard (an elite unit of the Byzantine army initially composed mainly of Norsemen). These hoards graphically illustrate the wealth of many of the inhabitants of Gotland during the early Viking period.

Viking hoards are much less common on the Swedish mainland, though there have been one or two interesting discoveries, the most important of which was found near Sweden's main international airport in 2008. In April of that year archaeologists from the Swedish National Heritage Board came upon a spectacular Viking silver hoard while excavating a Bronze Age tomb in the Steningehöjden, a residential area of Sigtuna, near Stockholm Arlanda Airport, Stockholm. Unusually, the treasure was found inside the burial chamber of the prehistoric tomb, which had stood there for at least 1,400 years before the Vikings Age. The cache consisted of 472 silver coins, most of which were minted in Baghdad in modern-day Iraq and Damascus in Syria, though some originated in Persia and North Africa. Most of the coins in the hoard had been cut into pieces, indicating that the Vikings valued them for their silver content rather than their monetary value. Kenneth Jonsson, a professor at the Stockholm Numismatic Institute, part of the archaeological department at the University of Stockholm, has dated the Arlanda airport hoard to about AD 850. This date shows that the Vikings were receiving foreign currency through overseas trade, or perhaps obtaining loot from raids, much earlier than previously thought. It is rare for Viking hoards to be deposited inside prehistoric monuments, and one can only speculate that perhaps these particular Vikings believed their ancestors would protect the hoard or even placed the treasure inside as an offering for their ancestors, not intending to recover it. However, bearing in mind that the prehistoric tomb would have been a prominent landmark in the area, it is also possible that the reason for the burial is more prosaic, and that the Vikings buried the cache there so it would be easy to find when they came back for it later.

# The Quedlinburg Hoard

The incredible story behind the Quedlinburg Hoard reads more like a movie script than a factual account. The hoard, a magnificent collection of medieval objects belonging to the Church of St. Servatius in Quedlinburg, in Germany's Harz Mountains, was looted by the Nazis during WW II and hidden in a mineshaft on the edge of the town. In April 1945, during the last weeks of the war, the town was occupied by American troops, and the cave and its contents were put under military guard. Nevertheless, it was soon discovered that many items from the treasure had disappeared from the cave. Despite intensive searches, no trace of the hoard was found and it seemed that the exquisite treasures it contained—estimated to be worth more than $200 million today—had disappeared forever. Then in the late 1980s, after an exhaustive investigation into the case, a *New York Times* reporter made the incredible claim that he had located the Quedlinburg Hoard in a farm town in northeastern Texas. If this was true, how did the treasure get there and where had it been for the previous 40 years?

Quedlinburg lies on the northern edge of the Harz mountain range in the west of Saxony-Anhalt, east-central Germany. The town was founded in the ninth century and is overflowing with buildings of vast historical interest and significance, including Quedlinburg Abbey (founded by Emperor Otto the Great in AD 936), several early Gothic churches, 14th-century fortifications, a 17th-century city hall, and 1,300 half-timbered houses.

*13.1. Castle and monastery of Quedlinburg. Image by Annabell Preußler. Licensed under the Creative Commons Attribution-Share Alike 3.0 Unported license on Wikipedia.*

The nucleus of the town, the castle/abbey/church complex, is situated on a sandstone cliff known as Castle Hill. Quedlinburg Abbey's church, the Collegiate Church of St. Servatius, is the resting place of the first German King Heinrich I (Henry the Fowler, AD 876–936) and his wife, Mathilde (AD 895–968), later canonized as Saint Mathilda. The original collegiate church of St. Servatius was constructed when King Heinrich established his residence on Castle Hill, but this building was partly destroyed by fire in 1070. After a massive rebuilding program, spanning the years 1070 to 1129, the church emerged as a magnificent example of Romanesque architecture. It also gained prestige and wealth due to its imperial connections, accumulating considerable treasures, among which were religious relics, works of art, and Byzantine artifacts given to Empress Theophanu (AD 955–983), wife of Holy Roman Emperor Oto II, as wedding gifts. In 1179, a church treasury was built into the northern part of the church transept and it is there that its splendid donations were subsequently kept. In recognition of Quedlinburg's architectural riches, UNESCO declared the entire town a World Heritage Site in 1994.

But there is a darker side to the town's history. On July 2, 1936 (the 1,000th anniversary of Heinrich I's death), Heinrich Himmler, the dreaded leader of the SS, the black-uniformed elite corps of Hitler's Nazi Party, organized an elaborate midnight ceremony in the crypt of Quedlinburg Abbey in which the bones of Heinrich I, which had supposedly been excavated by the Nazis, were solemnly reburied next to his wife, Queen Mathilde. Indeed Himmler, who was deeply involved in pseudo-occult activities, was deranged enough to believe he was the reincarnation of Heinrich I, Germany's first king and therefore, in the eyes of Himmler, the founding father of Nazism. For the duration WWII the Collegiate Church and castle at Quedlinburg were closed and converted into Nazi shrines. In 1943, threatened by continual Allied bombing, the Nazis decided that the Quedlinburg Abbey Treasure (like many others they looted at this time) should be removed and hidden from the Allies. Consequently, the treasure was taken to the edge of the town and hidden in a mine shaft (or mushroom cave, in some versions). On April 18, 1945, just two weeks before German surrender, U.S. forces in the form of the 87th Armored Field Infantry Battalion entered Quedlinburg. After surrendering the town, the Burgermeister apparently informed the U.S. commander of the location of the mineshaft and the treasure contained within it.

When the U.S. Army inspected the mineshaft along with local representatives of the Church, they found the treasure intact and posted guards at the entrance. However, a few days later there was another inspection, and it was discovered that several pieces from the hoard were missing. Although it seemed likely that American soldiers had taken the objects, nothing could be proven. Further investigations into the looting were undertaken, but these were severely hindered when Quedlinburg was occupied by the Red Army and incorporated into the Soviet Zone, eventually becoming part of East Germany in 1949. The Quedlinburg Treasure, it seems, had disappeared for good, and there was very little the U.S. Army or church officials could do about it.

But what exactly had been stolen from the mineshaft? Reported missing were a fantastic collection of art treasures and religious manuscripts, including three reliquaries of Saint Servatius, Saint Katharine, and Heinrich, all dating from c1200–1230. These reliquaries are rectangular boxes covered in gold with filigree work and are decorated with reliefs along the sides. The Servatius reliquary is also enhanced with a large amethyst. Also missing was a spectacular ninth-century illuminated manuscript gospel book, known as the "Samuhel Gospel." This manuscript of the four gospels, estimated to be worth up to $30 million today, is written in gold ink and encased in a jewel-encrusted gold and silver binding. It was donated to Quedlinburg Abbey by King Heinrich I. Other looted valuables included an ivory liturgical comb decorated with precious stones, dated to the seventh or eighth century; a large first-century AD alabaster jar, said to have been used at the wedding at Cana; a 10th-century crystal reliquary with gilded and jeweled mounts originating from Egypt or Syria, and donated by Emperor Otto III (AD 980–1002); a printed silver and jewel-covered evangeliary (book of gospel readings for services) dating to 1513; and gold and silver crucifixes. The art world and the church officials from Quedlinburg were convinced that this extraordinary medieval treasure had disappeared for good.

However, beginning in the late 1980s, there were signs that this was not so when the Samuhel Gospel appeared on the market in Europe, sparking a worldwide hunt for the remainder of the treasure. In 1989, William H. Honan, a senior reporter at the *New York Times,* together with German researcher Willi Korte, set out to discover the whereabouts of the treasure and the identity of the person who had stolen it. However, the pair initially met with a series of dead ends, and it seemed that after four decades the discovery of any new information about the hoard was extremely unlikely. But the investigators persevered, and, after combing through thousands of pages of old U.S. Army records and carrying out countless interviews and detailed investigations into the often shady dealings of the art world, they gathered enough information to relate an amazing tale of deception, daring, and intrigue. Indeed, the story they told the world was more akin to adventure fiction than truth.

In April 1945, Joe T. Meador was a 29-year-old lieutenant with the 87th when they occupied Quedlinburg. Meador had received a bachelor's degree in art from North Texas State University in 1938, so he would have had some knowledge of the value of the items secreted in the mineshaft that he and his colleagues had been ordered to guard. A number of soldiers from the 87th reported that they had seen Meador enter the mine shaft and leave carrying packages under his coat, though why no one seems to have reported this remains a mystery. Having stolen the treasures, Meador was said by witnesses to have put them in cardboard boxes (others said he wrapped them in brown paper) and sent them home to Whitewright, Texas, using military mail. Absurdly simple, yet obviously effective.

Meador was discharged from the Army in 1946 and returned home to Texas, where he taught art at a school in New London. But after his father became ill, Meador returned to his family home in Whitewright, where he helped his brother, Jack, run Meador Inc., the family hardware and farm equipment business. The only indication that Meador still had the treasure came one day in the hardware store when he showed employees two ancient richly bound gold and silver manuscripts as well as a number of other unusual art objects. Nothing else was heard of his incredible collection, and when Meador died in February 1980, his will listed real estate valued at $24,331 and stocks worth $81,225.57, but there was no mention of the Quedlinburg Hoard. Meador's will passed these assets on to his sister, Jane Meador Cook, who served as executor of his estate, and their brother, Jack. Whether Meador's brother and sister knew of the treasure is uncertain, but they soon realized that they had inherited something extraordinary and began arranging to sell the objects.

In 1983 Meador's brother-in-law, Dr. Don H. Cook, a dentist practicing in Mesquite, Texas, asked Dallas estate appraiser John Carroll Collins to evaluate "two old books."[1] Collins had studied medieval manuscripts for two years as a graduate student at North Texas State University and immediately recognized that the "old books" were actually rare medieval manuscripts in jeweled bindings. Collins also noted the date on the back of one of the manuscripts (1513), the date of the more recent of the Quedlinburg manuscripts. Collins was not allowed to examine the manuscripts closely or to take any photographs, and after the meeting heard nothing more until March 1986, when his expertise was called upon again. At this meeting members of Meador's family were present and Collins was allowed to arrange to have the manuscripts photographed. But this appointment was canceled, and Collins never heard from the Meadors again.

Toward the end of 1985, Jack Meador, along with his son, Jeff, approached Decherd H. Turner, director of the Humanities Research Center at the University of Texas in Austin, and showed him slides of two medieval manuscripts that they were trying to sell. The astonished Turner asked the pair where they had obtained such rare manuscripts, and Jack replied that his brother had found them in the gutter in Germany at the end of the War. Jack arranged for Turner to fly to Dallas to examine the manuscripts and possibly make an offer on them, but Jeff Meador canceled the trip at the last moment without saying why. Convinced that what he had seen were the Quedlinburg manuscripts, Turner phoned Jeff Meador at his home, only to be told that the manuscripts had already been sold and that he should speak to

Jack Meador's lawyer, John S. Torigian. Turner subsequently met Torigian privately and offered to raise $1 million to buy back the manuscripts but was refused point blank.

Torigian had previously attempted to sell the manuscripts to Paul-Louis Couailhac, a rare book dealer in Paris. Couailhac said that he would try to sell the older of the two manuscripts for a staggering $9 million but afterward heard nothing from Torigian. He later found out that Torigian had actually sold the manuscript to West Germany's Cultural Foundation of the States, an organization established to repatriate lost German art, for a mere $3 million (which they referred to as a "finder's fee"), through a Bavarian art dealer named Heribert Tenschert. This transaction was finalized in May 1990, but news of the sale had drawn the attention not only of the West German government but also agencies of the U.S. government, including the IRS and the FBI. One of the results of subsequent investigations into the sale was that on June 18, 1990, the Lutheran church in Quedlinburg filed a lawsuit in Texas in an attempt to recover the artifacts it believed to have been stolen by Joe T. Meador in 1945.

Despite the evidence against their brother, Joe Meador's heirs contested ownership of the valuable artifacts and months of legal wrangling followed, during which time the treasure was moved from the First National Bank of Whitewright, where the Meadors had deposited it, to a neutral location at the Dallas Museum of Art. Fortunately for the Meadors, the statute of limitations in Texas is only two years, so a negotiated settlement was agreed upon. On January 7, 1991, both parties announced that they had reached an agreement (though this was not finally signed until February 26, 1992) that the Meador family would be paid $1 million for the return of all the artifacts to Germany. The Quedlinburg Treasure subsequently went on public display at the Dallas Museum of Art from March 7, 1992, to April 26, 1992, before being returned to Germany, where it was exhibited in Munich and Berlin, and eventually returned home to Quedlinburg in 1993. Since that time, artifacts from the Quedlinburg Treasure have been on display in the collegiate church St. Servatius.

The U.S. government was not finished with the Meador family, and, in January 1996, they and their former attorney, John Torigian, were indicted on charges of conspiring to sell the Samuhel Gospel and the Evangelistar. If found guilty, the defendants could have faced maximum prison sentences of 10 years and a fine of up to $250,000. But luck was on their side, and two years later a federal judge dismissed the indictments on a technicality. However, shortly after the federal case was dismissed, the IRS made a claim for more than $50 million in taxes, penalties, and interest from the family. Again the Meadors got lucky, and in April 2000, they escaped with only having to pay the IRS $135,000. In May 2003, Jack Meador died at the age of 83, followed in July of the same year by his sister, Jane, at the age of 71.

This incredible story does not quite end there. Representatives of the Church Quedlinburg have stated that some objects from the treasure remain unaccounted for. Thomas R. Kline, now a litigation partner with law firm Andrews Kurth, represented the Quedlinburg church in the federal case of 1990 and believes that two pieces from the hoard (a crystal reliquary shaped like a bishop's hat and a hollow gold cross) are still in the Dallas area. Indeed, attorney Alan Harris, who also represented the Quedlinburg church in the case, once received a phone call from a woman whom he is convinced was in possession of the hollow gold cross. There is also the tantalizing possibility that Joe T. Meador was not the only one taking pieces of the Quedlinburg Treasure out of the mineshaft in 1945; other U.S. soldiers or even Soviet or German troops may also have looted some of the objects. Perhaps one day somewhere in the dark world of illegal antiquities other pieces from this exquisite medieval collection will surface and hopefully find their way back home to the Church of St. Servatius.

*The Search for the Ancient Chinese Treasure Ships*

Traditional and popular accounts of the incredible early-15th-century voyages of Chinese eunuch admiral Zheng He describe fleets of vast nine-masted wooden vessels journeying to Arabia, Brunei, the Horn of Africa, India, Southeast Asia, and Thailand. On these expeditions the Chinese traded gold, silver, porcelain, and silk, and in return received ostriches, zebras, camels, ivory, and even a giraffe from Swahili. During this period the Chinese were also looking to expand their influence beyond India and Africa, and if the Ming emperors had continued their investment in the treasure fleets, there may have been Chinese colonies springing up throughout the world, rather than Portuguese, Spanish, Dutch, and British. But this never happened, the priorities of the Chinese court changed, the treasure junks were decommissioned, and maritime trade was eventually banned. What happened to cause this change in attitude, and what might world history have been like if the voyages of the Chinese treasure ships had continued? And what of the treasure ships themselves? If descriptions of these huge vessels are accurate, they would have been the largest wooden ships ever constructed; indeed Christopher Columbus's flagship, the *Santa Maria*, would only have been one-fifth the size of the largest treasure ship. However, some researchers disagree as to the accuracy and interpretation of the medieval Chinese sources, and consider the descriptions and dimensions of the treasure ships greatly exaggerated. How big were these treasure ships, and what happened to them?

14.1. *A full-size model of a middle-sized treasure boat of the Zheng He fleet at the Treasure Boat Shipyard site in Nanjing. Photo by Vmenkov. Licensed under the Creative Commons Attribution-Share Alike 3.0 Unported, 2.5 Generic, 2.0 Generic and 1.0 Generic license on Wikipedia.*

The main sources for Zheng He's extraordinary voyages are the imperial annals of the Ming dynasty emperors (1368–1644), collectively known as the *Ming Shilu* (*Veritable Records of the Ming*); the *Ying-Yai Sheng-Lan* (*Overall Survey of the Ocean's Shores*), written in 1433 by Ma Huan, a Muslim traveler and translator who accompanied Admiral Zheng He on three of his seven expeditions; and the *Xin Cha Shen Lan* (*Description of the Starry Raft*), written in 1436 by Fei Xin, a Chinese Muslim and Arabic scholar who had participated in the third, fifth, and seventh expeditions. Further information about Zheng He's maritime expeditions can be gleaned from his inscriptions on stone monuments, such as that carved in 1431 at a temple to a Taoist goddess called the Celestial Spouse at Changle in Fujian Province, which records his veneration for the goddess and gives details of his voyages.

Although Zheng He's fleet and voyages were indeed extraordinary, they were not without precedent. The Chinese had a long history of maritime trade and were building oceangoing trade ships as far back as the Song Dynasty (AD 960–1270). The succeeding Mongol emperors of the Yuan Dynasty (c AD 1271–AD 1368) constructed larger seagoing trading vessels and founded trading posts in Sumatra, Ceylon, and southern India. Venetian merchant Marco Polo (c AD 1254–AD 1324) stayed at the Mongol court from 1275 to 1292, and described four-masted, seagoing merchant vessels with watertight bulkheads, 60 individual cabins for merchants, and crews of up to 300. In the second half of the 14th century, the Han Chinese overthrew the Mongols and founded the Ming Dynasty (AD 1368–1644), taking over the fleet and a long-established, well-mapped trade network.

In 1402, Zhu Di, Prince of Yan, usurped the Chinese throne and became known to history as the Yongle emperor (posthumously titled Emperor Ming Chengzu). An eager supporter of maritime commerce, the Yongle emperor ordered all coastal shipyards to begin the construction of vessels to be part of a vast treasure fleet, the commander of which was to be a Muslim eunuch named Zheng He (AD 1371–1433), given the title "Admiral of the Western Seas" by the emperor. By 1405 around 1,180 ships of various types had been built. In the winter of that same year, the first fleet, one of the greatest ever assembled, comprising of more than 60 large "treasure" vessels and 255 smaller vessels, and with a total crew of more than 27,800 men, sailed from the Yangtze estuary in eastern China (modern Shanghai).

In organizing and sponsoring this huge naval expedition the Ming government was attempting to establish a Chinese presence in the Indian Ocean basin and impose imperial control over trade, partly by acquiring imperial vassals among the rulers of the area. Just as importantly, however, the huge flotilla of ships was showing "the barbarians" that Ming China was a force to be reckoned with in both commercial and military terms. It was also rumored that another purpose of the voyage was to locate Zhu Yunwen (the previous emperor, whom the Yongle emperor had usurped) and who was said to have fled into exile abroad. The theory was that if the Yongle emperor's potential rival to the throne was removed, then his position would be secure. However, to organize such a vast fleet of ships, containing huge quantities of trade goods, men, and supplies merely in order to seek out one man seems unlikely.

On this first voyage Zheng He led the ships southward to the rich kingdom of Champa (central Vietnam), on to Thailand, and then through the Strait of Malacca, a narrow, 500-mile stretch of water between the Malay Peninsula and the Indonesian island of Sumatra, then and now an important passageway between China and India. In these treacherous waters Zheng He's fleet was attacked by an infamous Chinese pirate called Chen Zuyi and allegedly lost 5,000 men before finally overcoming him and taking him prisoner. Even today the Strait of Malacca has a high rate of piracy; in 2004, for example, the area accounted for 40 percent of piracy worldwide, though since that date an increase in sea and air patrols has decreased the problem.[1]

After the battle with Chen Zuyi, Zheng He sailed into the Indian Ocean, where the ships encountered a hurricane that almost destroyed the fleet. According to records, the sailors believed all was lost and began praying to the Celestial Spouse. Suddenly a "divine light" appeared at the tips of the mast and the danger subsided. This strange light was probably St. Elmo's fire, a weather phenomenon caused by static electricity, which sometimes appears on the masts of ships and the wings of airplanes.

The fleet then went on to India and Sri Lanka before returning to China in 1407. The first of what would become collectively known as the Voyages of Zheng He or Voyages of Cheng Ho had been a success, with control of the Straits of Malacca now in Chinese hands (Chen Zuyi was executed after the fleet returned to China) and the Ming government in possession of a far greater knowledge of the outside world.

Between 1407 and 1433 there were six more voyages, the earliest of which visited ports around the Indian Ocean where Chinese silk, porcelain, and lacquer ware were traded for medicinal herbs, spices, ivory, rare woods, and pearls to bring back to the imperial court. Zheng He's fourth voyage (1414–1415) was far more ambitious than the previous expeditions, reaching as far as the Persian Gulf and Arabia. In Hormuz, on the Persian Gulf, Zheng obtained precious stones and metals, while other ships from the fleet sailed to the kingdom of Bengal in present-day Bangladesh. Here the Chinese procured a giraffe, which had been sent as a gift to India from a ruler in Swahili, east Africa. When the fleet returned home in 1415 the giraffe was presented at court in Nanjing where the emperor's advisors identified it as the Qilin, a fabled unicorn-like creature associated with an age of peace and prosperity. So auspicious was the arrival of this strange magical creature that Zheng He arranged for another giraffe to be sent from Africa.

The final three voyages, which took place between 1416 and 1433, explored the east African coast, reaching Malindi in Kenya and possibly even Madagascar. While in eastern Africa the Chinese obtained more exotic animals for the emperor, including lions, leopards, "camel-birds" (ostriches), and "celestial horses" (zebras), and learned more details about Europe from Arab traders. But could Zheng He and his fleet have traveled even farther than Africa? In his 2002 bestseller *1421: The Year China Discovered America,* Gavin Menzies, a retired British submarine lieutenant-commander, put forward the extravagant theory that, unknown to the rest of the world, the Chinese had also rounded the Cape of Good Hope and reached as far as America more than 70 years before Columbus. According to Menzies, the fleet then circumnavigated the globe before landing in Australia. Although Menzies's theory was popular for a while, after examining Menzies's case closely, a number of scholars and navigators, such as historian Robert Finlay and master mariner Captain Philip J. Rivers, concluded that there was not a single artifact or document to support such a voyage by the Ming fleets.

Despite Menzies's fantasies, Chinese maritime trade and commercial activity, as well as their nautical knowledge and technology, were at their height at the time of Zheng He's fifth and sixth voyages (1416–1422). These achievements were decades before most of the famous European voyages of discovery: Christopher Columbus (America, 1492,); Vasco da Gama (the first European to reach India, in 1498); and Ferdinand Magellan (the first documented circumnavigation of the globe, 1519–1522). So, why did Ming China's success not lead to significant commercial maritime expansion into the Middle East and beyond Africa into Europe? The fact that China did not expand on these voyages meant that it would remain relatively isolated, leaving European explorers to extend their influence into Africa and Asia without competition.

There are a number of theories as to why the Chinese did not grasp this seemingly golden opportunity. The first was the massive cost involved in financing such huge maritime ventures. The lavish nature of Zheng He's voyages had become the subject of heated debate among rival factions at the Ming Court, and in May 1421, toward the end of the reign of the Yongle emperor, it was ordered that they be suspended due to their expense. But the order seems to have come too late to affect Zheng He's sixth voyage, which set sail in March 1421. Nevertheless, when the successor of the Yongle emperor, Zhu Gaochi (reigned AD 1424–1425 under the title Hongxi) came to power, he immediately brought an end to Zheng He's maritime expeditions. But cost was probably not the only reason for this decision. The reopening of the Grand Canal in 1411 also played its part. Starting at Beijing and running for 1,104 miles to the city of Hangzhou in Eastern China, the Grand Canal is the longest canal in the world. After the Canal was completely renovated between 1411 and 1415, it provided a quicker and safer route for transporting grain than seagoing vessels traveling along the coast.

In June 1431, Zheng He managed to undertake one final voyage under the rule of Hongxi's son, the Xuande emperor (reigned AD 1426–1435). The last expedition sailed to Africa's Swahili coast and reached as far as the Cape of Good Hope, but in 1433 on the way back to China, Zheng He, then in his 60s, died and was buried at sea. With the death of the "Admiral of the Western Seas" came the end of China's golden age of exploration. Now the conservative Confucian faction had the upper hand at court; there would be no more maritime voyages, Zheng He's Treasure Ships were said to have been burned or left to rot away in their harbors, and official records of the voyages were destroyed.

Throughout the last few decades there has been heated discussion among scholars and laymen alike as to the dimensions of Zheng He's treasure ships (called *baoshan* in the ancient texts). Are the ancient Chinese records accurate in their descriptions of these seemingly colossal vessels? The largest ships in the fleet are recorded as being nine masted, with four decks, and measuring between 440 and 538 feet long by 210 feet wide—much larger than any wooden ship ever built. Some scholars regard these dimensions as inaccurate, as such huge vessels would be impractical and structurally unsound. This is evidenced, for example, by the huge wooden warships of the British Victorian age, such as the HMS *Orlando* and HMS *Mersey* (both 336 feet in length), which due to their size suffered from structural problems that required internal iron strapping to support the hull. Because there is no mention of such special construction techniques in the Chinese records, how were such huge vessels constructed? Were the ancient texts describing real seagoing vessels or some kind of mythological craft?

One explanation is that the oceangoing treasure ships that the Ming Dynasty constructed were much smaller in size than described in the texts. Massive vessels of the size mentioned in the ancient Chinese annals may also have been built, but as river craft to be used by the emperor and imperial bureaucrats to travel along the Yangtze, which could have been navigable for such large ships. Such flat-bottomed estuarine vessels were known as *shachuan,* and perhaps journeys down the river by the emperor and his revenue on these huge elaborate vessels were intended as lavish displays of imperial power.

Dr. Richard Gould, professor of archeology at Brown University, in Providence, Rhode Island (United States), believes that the unrealistic sizes of the treasure ships may be due to the known extravagances of the Yongle emperor Zhu Di. This extravagance is well illustrated by the emperor's plan to erect a 240-feet-high stone tablet in his father's tomb (known as the Ming Xiaoling Mausoleum). The vast monument proved so unwieldy that the project was abandoned and the various parts of the stele were left lying in Yangshan Quarry, where they remain today. Zhu Di was forced to order the construction of a much smaller tablet to be installed in the tomb. Are there perhaps echoes of the grandiose ideas behind the huge treasure ships and their marathon expeditions in the Yongle emperor's elaborate plans for his father's tomb? But whether built as seagoing treasure ships or as river craft primarily for display purposes, is there any convincing archaeological evidence for the existence of these huge vessels?

In 1962 a timber rudder post more than 36 feet long and 1.25 feet in diameter was unearthed amongst the remains of the Ming boatyards in Nanjing. Researchers calculated that a rudder of such a size must have come from a ship of at least 450 feet in length, indicating that huge vessels were indeed constructed there. Unfortunately, apart from this tantalizing glimpse of what may have been part of a treasure ship, any more substantial archeological traces of China's golden age of exploration remain elusive; only three of Nanjing's seven ship docks where the Ming ships were constructed remain today, and only one of these has been excavated.

Nevertheless, there is archaeological evidence from ship-wrecks of other periods that Zheng He's voyages would have been possible. In 1973, during canal dredging work at Houzhou, six miles from the ancient trading port of Quanzhou, in southern Fujian province, the remains of a large ship were found buried in the mud. Known as the Quanzhou Wreck, the ship probably sank in the 1270s (the earlier Song period) and was a substantial double-masted seagoing vessel, about 114 feet long by 32 feet wide. Excavations led by Zhuang Weij, professor of history at Xiamen University, took place in 1974, and revealed compartments inside the ship containing 504 copper coins, an exotic cargo of spices (including frankincense possibly from Arabia and black pepper from Java), cowrie shells, tortoiseshell, ambergris (from Somalia), betel nuts from Indonesia, and about 5,000 pounds of fragrant woods. Archaeological examination of the Quanzhou Wreck and its cargo suggested that the ship was an oceangoing merchant vessel returning to Quanzhou from Southeast Asia, evidence that the Chinese were already involved in long-distance trading voyages across the Indian Ocean a century before the Ming Dynasty. The remains of the Quanzhou ship are now preserved in Quanzhou Overseas Relations Museum.

A wreck that dates from a little later than the Quanzhou Wreck was excavated between 1976 and 1982 near Shinan, South Korea. Unfortunately divers had looted the site before government authorities put it under protection, though a substantial amount of important information could still be gleaned from the wreck. The ship, which dated from around 1323, was carrying cargo that included at least 16,000 ceramic items, including bluish white porcelain from the Mongolian Yuan Dynasty (AD 1271–1368), pieces of red sandalwood, and more than seven million brass-bronze coins. Further study showed that the vessel was constructed of Chinese red fir and Chinese red pine, and was similar in size and construction to the Quanzhou wreck. Archaeologists concluded that it was a Chinese merchant ship en route from China to Japan when it sank in a storm.

A more recent find was that of the wreck known as the Nan'ao No. 1, off the coast of Shantou, in Guangdong Province in southern China. Discovered in 2007 by a group of fishermen, this merchant ship, which measured 84 feet in length and 23 feet in width, has been dated to the reign of Emperor Wanli (AD 1573–1620), late in the Ming Dynasty. Nan'ao No. 1 is considered the best preserved ancient shipwreck in China, and excavations have revealed that most of the cargo was Ming porcelain for export, indicating the importance of the port of Shantou on what has become known as the Maritime Silk Road. The Maritime Silk Road was a sea route dating back to the Eastern Han Dynasty (AD 25–220), which connected China to India, the Red Sea, the Persian Gulf, and the Mediterranean. Between 2004 and 2009 a research project named "908," sponsored by the State Oceanic Administration's Department of Science and Technology, scoured the coast of China for ancient shipwrecks associated with the route. Although the project was a success and revealed 30 shipwreck sites scattered along the shores of China, none of these were connected with Zheng He's expeditions. In fact, as can be seen from the shipwrecks discussed previously, Chinese wrecks tend to date from either significantly earlier or later than the voyages of Zheng He's treasure ships.

So does the lack of archaeological evidence mean that Zheng He's treasure fleets never existed as described in ancient Chinese texts? Without further underwater survey and archaeological excavation, it is impossible to be sure. But whether the literal truth or not, stories of the fantastic voyages of the treasure ships of the Ming Empire have captured popular imagination the world over. In 2006 it was announced that a 233.3-foot replica of a treasure ship was to be constructed in Nanjing, with a $10 million budget and a three-year timeline. The ship is being built using 15th-century construction methods and ancient wooden shells made from oak trees, though it will also be equipped three engines, computers, and central air conditioning. In 2010, the press was shown pictures of the replica in the process of construction in Nanjing, and it was announced that vessel would be ready for sailing by 2014.

The legacy of Zheng He's treasure fleet is not only present in this reconstruction, but also in the various inscriptions he left behind. In 1431, just before departing on what was to be his final voyage, Zheng He, inscribed a stele in Fujian province, part of which reads:

> We have traversed more than one hundred thousand li [a *li* is about one-third of a mile] of immense water spaces and have beheld in the ocean huge waves like mountains rising sky-high, and we have set eyes on barbarian regions far away hidden in a blue transparency of light vapors, while our sails loftily unfurled like clouds day and night continued their course (rapid like that) of a star, traversing those savage waves as if we were treading a public thoroughfare. Truly this was due to the majesty and the good fortune of the Court and moreover we owe it to the protecting virtue of the divine Celestial Spouse.[2]

*The Spanish Treasure Fleet*

The Spanish Treasure Fleets sailed the ocean from the New World to Spain from the 16th to the 18th centuries carrying a wide variety of goods from the colonies. Their cargo included tobacco, spices, pearls, and gems, as well as gold and silver taken from the Aztecs and Incas. With such rich treasures, the ships soon became targets for English, Dutch, and French warships, and a number of them were looted on their long journey back from the Americas. But the most serious threat to the Spanish Treasure Fleets was the weather, particularly hurricanes. Numerous vessels were lost during severe storms, particularly along the coasts of Vera Cruz (in modern Mexico), Texas, and Florida. One of the best known of these wrecks is that of the *Nuestra Senora de Atocha*, which sank off the Florida coast in 1622 carrying around 35 tons of silver and more than 160 pieces of gold, as well as copper, tobacco, and jewels. In July 1715, all 11 ships of the Spanish Treasure Fleet were destroyed in a hurricane near present-day Vero Beach, Florida. Beginning in the mid-20th century various treasure divers and salvage companies have attempted to retrieve the treasure hoards from the sea bed, sometimes with remarkable success. But many of these trea-sure hunters have come under intense criticism from archaeolo-gists both for their crude methods of recovery and their thirst for wealth rather than for knowledge.

The arrival of Christopher Columbus in the Bahamas in 1492 signaled the beginning of Spain's Empire in the New World, which would expand over the next 400 years to cover most of modern Central America and Mexico, the Caribbean islands, the western half of South America, and a large part of North America. The basis for Spain's New World Empire was the exploitation of the wealth of the conquered kingdoms, particularly their gold and silver. These precious metals were of vital importance to Spain, as they could be melted down to make desperately needed currency in the form of gold and silver coins. In 1535, Spain established the first mint in the Americas in Mexico City, which produced coins for domestic use, though Spanish coins from the New World did not start entering world circulation until two decades later. After the conquest of the Inca Empire under Francisco Pizarro in the 1530s, the amount of wealth, particularly gold and silver stolen from the natives, arriving in Spain from the New World increased dramatically. The Spanish king, Charles I, ordered that all of the gold ornaments and jewelry from the Americas be melted down and made into *escudos* (gold coins), destroying a huge part of Inca culture in the process.

The Spanish had been shipping goods back to Spain in mer-chant vessels from the Americas since the time of Columbus, but attacks on the ships by French-backed privateers as they arrived in Spanish ports persuaded the government that something had to be done to protect their wealth. Beginning in 1522, the Span-ish government organized a fleet of warships that was sent into the Atlantic Ocean to protect the returning merchant ships as they sailed into port with their precious cargo. In response to the increasingly large amounts of gold and silver from the conquered Inca Empire carried by Spanish ships, the French now sent their privateers further out into the Atlantic, a long way from Span-ish waters. As a result, in 1537 the French captured nine treasure ships, forcing the Spanish government to send a fleet of royal warships out as far as the Caribbean to escort the remaining vessels back to port in Spain. It is this convoy of merchant vessels and warships that is considered to represent the first real Treasure Fleet.

In 1545 the Spanish discovered silver ore at the Cerro Rico ("Rich Mountain") in southwest Bolivia. On April 10, 1545, the mining town of Potosi was founded at the foot of the Cerro Rico, and the mines became the major source of silver for Spain's empire in the New World. Indeed the mines here were so rich that Potosi expanded rapidly to become one of the largest cities in the Americas with a population of more than 200,000 people. The mines at Cerro Rico were to have a huge effect on world economy, as the vast amounts of silver loaded on board the treasure ships and taken to Spain resulted in Spanish currency flooding the market.

*15.1. Silver peso of Philip V. Courtesy of Wikipedia.*

By 1550 the Treasure Fleet numbered 17 ships, but after the French pirate Jacques de Sores attacked and burned the trading port of Havana in 1555, the new king of Spain, Philip II, decided that something more substantial and organized was necessary. The king consulted admiral and explorer Pedro Menéndez de Avilés (1519–1574), best known today as the founder of the city of St. Augustine, Florida, in 1565. De Avilés had been the commander of vessels that had escorted the Treasure Fleet on previous occasions and so he was well qualified to make recommendations to the king about how the Fleet might be organized in the future. In 1564 the Council of the Indies in Madrid (an organization established to oversee Spain's colonial empire) drew up a basic formal plan to demonstrate how the shipments of precious metals mined in the New World could be protected from pirates and colonial rivals on their journey back to Spain.

*15.2. Woodcut carving of Pedro Menendez de Avilés, 1923. Courtesy of Wikipedia.*

The Council decided to organize the ships into two huge convoys known as the *Tierra Firme* (South America) Fleet and the *Nueva España* (New Spain–Mexican) Fleet, with both convoys including merchant ships, war ships, supply ships, and reconnaissance vessels. The departures of the fleets were scheduled to avoid the hurricane season and take advantage of winds and currents. Each fleet usually traveled separately, in convoys of between 30 and 90 vessels, at different times to minimize losses to the weather or pirates, though occasionally they journeyed as far as the Caribbean together before going their separate ways. The merchant vessels were loaded with supplies of European goods such as wine, olive oil, textiles, tools, and weapons, to sell or trade with the colonists. The *Tierra Firme* Fleet would sail from Seville in the late summer bound for Cartagena de Indias ("Cartegina of the Indies") on the northern coast of Colombia, a journey that took from four to six weeks. On arrival at Cartagena, the Spanish would wait for about two months for the gold, silver, jewels, and spices collected from its southern colonies to be transported to the port and assembled, and be ready for export. From Cartagena the *Tierra Firme* Fleet sailed on to Havana, where the Spanish had established a large shipyard where any repairs necessary could be carried out before the voyage home across the Atlantic.

The *Nueva España* Fleet departed Spain in the spring on a two-month-long journey to the port of Vera Cruz, in present-day Mexico. After the arrival of the ships there would be a large trade fair, where the Spanish merchants from the fleet would trade their European goods for precious metals, emeralds, animal hides, sugar, and indigo. After the fair was over, the ships were loaded up and the convoy sailed along the coast of the Gulf of Mexico, until it reached Havana, where it rendezvoused with the *Tierra Firme* Fleet. The two convoys then left Havana together for their long journey across the Atlantic, sailing along the east coast of Florida and riding the Gulf Stream to Cape Hatteras, on the coast of North Carolina, where they turned eastward toward Spain. But before they made port in Spain, the Spanish convoys faced numerous hazards. Apart from hurricanes and pirates, the Fleets were faced with the problems of exhausted crew members, tropical diseases, malnutrition, and the extremely unhygienic conditions on board. Nevertheless, by the end of the 16th century, the Treasure Fleets had helped to make Spain the richest country in Europe—though it would soon have major rivals in the New World.

In 1621 the Dutch established the Dutch West India Company, a chartered company of Dutch merchants formed partly to develop the country's claims in the Americas. One of the major successes of the Company was the 1628 attack led by Dutch naval officer Pieter Pietersen Heyn (1577–1629) on a Spanish fleet loaded with silver from the American colonies. The battle took place in the Bay of Matanzas, on the northern coast of Cuba, and the Dutch took a total of 90 tons of gold and silver from the Spanish vessels. The Spanish hold on the New World was further weakened in 1634, when the Dutch took possession of Curaçao, a strategically important island in the southern Caribbean Sea, off the Venezuelan coast. The English were another colonial rival, and in 1655 invaded and captured the Caribbean island of Jamaica from Spain. Two years later, on April 20, 1657, a British fleet under Admiral Robert Blake (1598–1657) attacked and destroyed a fleet of 16 Spanish treasure ships in Santa Cruz Bay, Tenerife, in the Canary Islands. In the late 1650s the French began colonizing the major Caribbean island of Hispaniola and in 1664 established the colony of Saint-Domingue. Despite the occasional losses, however, it was rare for a Treasure Fleet to be destroyed or captured by enemy vessels.

By the 1650s the average number of ships in a Treasure Fleet had fallen to 25, and by 1700 Spain's power in the New World was lessening. Factors that contributed to this were the crippling cost of incessant wars with colonial rivals England, Holland, and France, and the decline in silver production at colonial mines such as Potosi. At the Battle of Vigo Bay, in Galicia, northwest Spain, in October 1702, the Treasure Fleet was attacked by an Anglo-Dutch fleet commanded by Admiral Sir George Rooke (1650–1709). The Treasure Fleet was destroyed, and the English and Dutch recovered about £14,000 worth of silver, though the majority of the cargo had already been unloaded by the Spanish and taken away before the battle. The Battle of Vigo Bay was fought at the beginning of the War of the Spanish Succession (1701–1714), a war caused by the disputed succession to the Spanish throne. Another confrontation that was part of this war took place on the small island of Pequeña Barú, (modern Isla El Rosario), 30 miles away from Cartagena. This battle, known as Wager's Action (after British Admiral Sir Charles Wager; 1666–1743), resulted in the loss of three Spanish ships from the Treasure Fleet. One of the vessels lost was the *San José,* which sank to the bottom of Caribbean, taking with it 589 crew and passengers, and a treasure of gold and silver estimated to be worth between $150 and $450 million today.

In 1778, King Charles III established the "Decree of Free Trade," which allowed Spanish colonies to trade directly with each other and with some ports in Spain, such as Barcelona and Alicante. After this decree the monopoly of the treasure ships on colonial trade was practically ended, and the Treasure Fleet convoys sailed the Atlantic no more.

But what remains today, if anything, of these once great galleons that crisscrossed the Atlantic three or four hundred years ago? Perhaps the most dangerous threat to the treasure ship convoys were hurricanes, and one of the worst areas on the convoy's route for such storms was off the Florida coast. The most famous of the Spanish Treasure Fleets devastated by hurricanes in this area were those of 1622 and 1715.

On September 4, 1622, the *Nuestra Señora de Atocha* (*Our Lady of Atocha*) sailed from Havana as part of a Treasure Fleet of 28 galleons that was departing weeks behind schedule. The *Atocha* carried an incredibly rich cargo, which included 24 tons of silver bullion, 180,00 pesos of silver coins, 582 copper ingots, 125 gold bars and discs, 350 chests of indigo, 525 bales of tobacco, 20 bronze cannon, 1,200 pounds of worked silverware, and 70 pounds of emeralds. On September 6th, the *Atocha* and seven other ships in the convoy encountered severe hurricanes off the Florida Coast and were driven onto the coral reefs near the Dry Tortugas, a small group of islands located at the end of the Florida Keys. The vessels were smashed to pieces on the rocks and quickly sank to the ocean floor, leaving only five survivors from the *Atocha*—three sailors and two slaves who had clung on to part of the mizzenmast (the third mast of a three-masted ship), the only part of the ship that remained on the surface of the ocean. The *Atocha* eventually came to rest about 55 feet below the surface, making a retrieval operation extremely difficult. A further hurricane in October of the same year inflicted more damage, scattering pieces of the wreck all over the ocean floor and making salvage practically impossible.

The loss of the *Atocha* came at a bad time for Spain. The Thirty Years' War (1618–1648) was still raging, and the country had borrowed heavily from foreign moneylenders to finance its role in the hostilities. But although the Spanish were able to locate almost half of the contents from another ship from the convoy, the *Santa Margarita,* they were never able to find any trace of the wreck of the *Atocha.*

On July 31, 1715, seven days after a long-delayed departure from Havana, the Spanish *Tierra Firme* Fleet of 11 ships, under the command of Captain-General Don Antonio de Escheverz y Zubiza and including the vessels the *Capitana,* the *Almiranta,* and the *Nuestra Senora de la Concepcion,* ran into a terrific hurricane near present-day Vero Beach, on the east coast of Florida. The colossal force of the hurricane smashed the ships to pieces on the jagged reefs just to the south of Cape Canaveral, sending the entire Treasure Fleet to the bottom of the ocean. Although there were some survivors, about 700 sailors were drowned, and lost with them was the Fleet's cargo, which included gold and silver bars and coins, jewelry, emeralds, pearls, and Chinese porcelain. The hurricane had scattered the wrecks of the Fleet over several miles, making salvage particularly difficult, though the Spanish did eventually manage to recover about half of the treasure. News of the disaster quickly spread and brought a host of privateers, pirates, and looters to the wreck site. One of these was British privateer Henry Jennings (died 1745), whose fleet attacked and looted the Spanish salvage camp at Palmar de Ayes (near modern Sebastian, Florida), and escaped with 120,000 pieces of eight (Spanish silver coins) and various other valuables including two bronze cannons.

Despite numerous salvage attempts, which continued with varying success until 1718, a large amount of the Treasure Fleet's cargo still remained at the bottom of the ocean. Gradually the disaster was forgotten, and it was not until well into the 20th century, with the development of the scuba in the 1950s and stories of silver coins from the Treasure Fleet being washed up on Florida beaches, that any attempt was made to hunt for the wrecked flotilla. In the 1950s a building contractor named Kip Wagner became interested in the wreck of the 1715 Fleet after finding coins belonging to the treasure ships on the beaches around the city of Sebastian. Wagner went on to form a treasure hunting and salvage group called the Real Eight Company. Early in 1961 Real Eight Company divers located a number of cannons from the 1715 Fleet and thousands of 1715 mint-marked Spanish coins. In 1963 Wagner was joined by a former chicken farmer named Mel Fisher, who had formed his own treasure hunting company called Treasure Salvors Inc. Together the two companies uncovered huge amount of treasure from the 1715 Fleet, including gold coins, jewelry, silver coins and bullion, Chinese porcelain, and numerous other artifacts. By the end of the 1960s the 1715 treasure ships had earned the two salvage companies more than $20 million, and Kip Wagner became a treasure hunting millionaire.

Locating the 1715 Fleet gave Mel Fisher treasure hunting fever, and he became fascinated at the possibility of locating the fabulous treasure carried by the *Nuestra Seora de Atocha,* lost off the Florida coast three and a half centuries earlier. His search of the area around Key West began in 1969, but it was not until 1980 that Fisher and Treasure Salvors Inc. recovered the remains of the *Santa Margarita,* the *Atocha*'s sister ship. Finally, in July 1985, the wreck of the fabled *Atocha,* along with its vast cargo of treasure from the New World, was discovered in the Lower Florida Keys and excavations under Duncan Mathewson, Fisher's chief archaeologist, got underway. But matters had not been so straightforward. Before the discovery of the *Atocha,* the State of Florida had made its own claims on the wreck site and eight years of litigation followed over the question of ownership of the *Atocha*'s treasure. Eventually, in 1982, after going all the way to the Supreme Court, Fisher agreed to a contract where 25 percent of the treasure went to the state of Florida.[1] Today the incredible artifacts from the ships of the 1622 Treasure Fleet, including an exquisite emerald and gold ring discovered from the wreck site as recently as 2011, are displayed as part of Mel Fisher Maritime Heritage Society Museum's collection in Key West.

Despite the excitement of the discoveries of the 1622 and 1715 wrecks, treasure hunters such as Mel Fisher and Kip Wagner are disapproved of by professional underwater archaeologists, due to their rudimentary salvage and recording techniques, and their habit of selling off the most valuable items from shipwrecks before they can be properly examined by museums. Although numerous Spanish wrecks have been salvaged in recent decades, and millions of dollars' worth of treasure uncovered and sold at auction, our knowledge of the size, weight, and design of the galleons of the Treasure Fleet has advanced little. Indeed, some of these wrecks have been practically destroyed by overzealous treasure hunters desperate to get at the wealth contained inside them. Archaeologists stress that the important difference between underwater archaeology and treasure hunting is that in the latter case the ultimate aim is to sell the recovered objects for personal gain, thus adding nothing to our knowledge of the artifacts in question and the culture that made and used them. But perhaps the establishment of museums like Mel Fishers Maritime Museum may show how salvage companies and archaeologists can work together to investigate and record important underwater shipwrecks like those of the Spanish Treasure Fleets, and thus further our understanding of the people that built and sailed these magnificent vessels.

## The Amber Room

The legendary Amber Room, an ornately decorated chamber made of amber panels backed with gold leaf, has been described by some as the Eighth Wonder of the World due to its exquisite craftsmanship. Created in the early 18th century by German and Russian artisans, the Amber Room was given as a gift to the Russian czar, Peter the Great, who had it installed in the Catherine Palace of Tsarskoye Selo near St. Petersburg, where it was to remain for the next 200 years. But in 1941, a few months after the Germans invaded Russia, Nazi soldiers looted the palace, packed up the Amber Room in crates, and shipped it to the German city of Königsberg, where it was put on display at the castle. After the city was bombed by the Royal Air Force in 1945, the Amber Room disappeared and entered into the realms of legend and hearsay. Some researchers believe the priceless treasure to have been destroyed in the bombing of Königsberg; others believe that it survives intact in a hidden bunker in the modern Russian city of Kaliningrad (previously the site of Königsberg), or was somehow spirited away to Berlin, Lithuania, or even America. The discovery of one of the panels of the Amber Room by German police in 1997 has persuaded many of the hundreds of treasure hunters on the trail of the great relic that stories of its demise during WWII have been greatly exaggerated, and that the fabulous wealth of the Amber Room (reputed to be around $150 million today) is still waiting to be discovered.

Located in Tsarskoye Selo ("Czar's Village"), a royal suburban estate now part of the town of Pushkin, 12 miles southeast of St. Petersburg, the Catherine Palace was the summer residence of the Russian czars. The first stone palace on the site was commissioned by Peter the Great for his wife, Catherine I (1684–1727), and built in 1717 as a two-story residence in late Baroque style by German architect Johann Friedrich Braunstein. The palace was substantially enlarged and modernized during the reign of Empress Elizabeth, the daughter of Peter the Great and Catherine I. Elizabeth engaged the court architect Bartolomeo Rastrelli to rebuild the palace in a highly ornate Rococo style. Her intention was that the scale of the Palace should rival Versailles, and by 1756 it had grown to more than half a mile in circumference. More than 220 pounds of gold were used to gild the stucco facade of the building and the numerous statues on its roof. Such opulent decoration and expenditure was not to everyone's taste, however.

Catherine II (1729–1796), better known as Catherine the Great, who became empress in 1762, regarded the decoration of the palace old fashioned and the financial outlay extravagant. Catherine made extensive changes to the palace in line with her Classical tastes; gilded parts were painted yellow, for example, and some of the interiors remodeled in Classical style. After Catherine's death in 1796, the throne passed to her son Paul I (reigned 1796–1801), with whom she had had a particularly bad relationship. On becoming the new czar, Paul closed the Catherine Palace and moved the royal residence to the palace at Pavlovsk, a couple of miles away. Future Russian monarchs resided in nearby Alexander Palace, which had been commissioned by Catherine the Great for her grandson, Alexander, who became emperor in 1801 after Paul I's assassination. The Alexander Palace was to be the summer residence of Russia's last ruling family, the Romanovs, and where they were placed under house arrest in 1917, before their execution in Yekaterinburg a year later.

Due to its golden color and its rarity, amber was extremely popular in the 18th century, and was often valued more highly than gold. Amber is a hard translucent fossilized resin produced by ancient trees that has been mined in the *Baltic* Sea region of northern Europe since prehistoric times. More than six tons of Baltic amber was used in the creation of the Amber Room. The Room was initially commissioned by the first king of Prussia (a historical region and former kingdom of north-central Europe, which included modern-day northern Germany and Poland), Frederick I (reigned 1701–1713), as a huge wall cover for a gallery at the Charlottenburg Palace, Berlin. The room was designed by German baroque sculptor Andreas Schlüter (1664–1714) and crafted by Danish master craftsman Gottfried Wolfram, with assistance from Gdańsk amber masters Ernst Schacht and Gottfried Turau. Work began in 1701 on what was to become 592.015 square feet of etched and mosaic amber panels backed with gold leaf and silver. Construction of the vast room is said to have taken 10 years, and we know that in 1716 Frederick William I, the son of Frederick I, who had died in 1713, gave the Amber Room as a gift to Czar Peter the Great, a diplomatic move that helped secure a Prussian-Russian alliance against Sweden, who had gained control of a large part of the Baltic region during the 17th and early 18th centuries.

But Peter the Great never got around to having the Amber Room reassembled, and the panels were kept in storage until his daughter Empress Elizabeth had it installed in the audience hall at the Winter Palace in St. Petersburg. In 1755 Elizabeth ordered the panels of the Amber Room be moved to Tsarskoje Selo, where she commissioned Italian-born Russian architect Francesco Bartolomeo Rastrelli to design a new Amber Room for the Catherine Palace. The Amber Room became Elizabeth's meditation room, the third of the chambers along the palace's exquisite Golden

Corridor, although the room was not finally completed until 1770. French writer Théophile Gautier described the Amber Room in his *Voyage en Russie* (1866):

> The room is rather large, with...walls wholly adorned with amber mosaic from top to bottom, including a frieze. The eye...is amazed and is blinded by the wealth and warmth of tints, representing all colours of the spectrum of yellow — from smoky topaz up to a light lemon.[1]

*16.1. The reconstruction of the Amber Room. Courtesy of Wikipedia.*

The Amber Room was restored and enlarged by Catherine the Great, who made it a meeting room for her intimate circle, and later Alexander II (1818–1881) used the room as a trophy room for his amber collection. Under Catherine the elaborate and entrancing room became the symbol of Imperial Russia and the monarch herself, the possessor of absolute power and limitless wealth. But there were practical problems. Due to the heat given off by the 565 candles that were lit to illuminate the exquisite room, the fragile wax binding used in its construction expanded and loosened over time. Consequently a caretaker was employed to maintain and repair the panels, and major restoration had to be carried out periodically during the 19th century. Nevertheless, for almost 200 years the Amber Room continued to be displayed in the Catherine Palace, and even in the mid-20th century remained one of the most famous rooms in Europe. But it was to be this fame that was ultimately to decide its fate.

On June 22, 1941, Adolf Hitler launched Operation Barbarossa, Germany's invasion of the Soviet Union, and one of the largest military operations in history in terms of both manpower and casualties. More than three million German troops and 3,400 tanks advanced into the Soviet Union in three groups, the north group heading for St. Petersburg (renamed Leningrad at the time), the center forces for Moscow, and the southern group into the Ukraine. Knowing what lay in store as the Nazis advanced on St. Petersburg, the curators at the Catherine Palace, which had been converted by Stalin into a state museum, made a desperate attempt to pack up as many valuable artifacts as possible and get them out of reach of the invaders. The Amber Room, however, proved more of a problem. When the officials responsible for removing the art treasures attempted to dismantle and remove the room, the fragile amber started to crumble in their hands. The amber had dried out and become brittle over the years, so it was almost impossible to move without destroying it. With no time to ponder alternatives, curator Anatoly Mikhailovich Kuchumov ordered that the amber panels be quickly covered in ordinary wallpaper in the hope that the German forces would not notice.

But when the Nazis arrived in Tsarskoye Selo in October 1941 armed with information given to them by their special team of art advisers known as the "Reichsleiter Rosenberg Taskforce" (named after Nazi intellectual Alfred Ernst Rosenberg), they knew exactly what they were looking for and where to find it. Items of Germanic origin such as the Amber Room were at the head of the Nazis' list, prepared before the invasion of the Soviet Union had even begun, and they were not going to leave without it. Within 36 hours the Amber Room was located, disassembled, and packed into 27 crates, and on October 27, 1941, Rittmeister Graf Solms-Laubach sent the cargo by train to Königsberg castle, on the Baltic Sea in East Prussia, the area from which it had originally come two centuries earlier. The issue of the newspaper *Königsberger Allgemeine Zeitung* for November 13, 1941, reported details of a display of part of the "Bernsteinzimmer" (Amber Room) in Königsberg castle. The Amber Room subsequently became an immensely popular exhibition at the castle museum and fell under the care of the museum's director Dr. Alfred Rohde, an amber connoisseur himself and the author of a treatise entitled "Amber, a German Material."

But as WWII progressed it became apparent that the Amber Room was in considerable danger at Königsberg castle. The Soviet Air Force had been making bombing raids on Königsberg since 1941, and in the summer of 1944 the town came under heavy attack from RAF Bomber Command, which would eventually destroy most of the city's historic quarters, including a large part of the castle. As Soviet forces approached the city toward the end of 1944 Dr. Alfred Rohde ordered the Amber Room to be dismantled yet again and stored in boxes in a more secure part of the castle, the Knights' Hall, in preparation for shipment to safety. One story goes that Erich Koch Gauleiter (party leader) of the Nazi Party in East Prussia managed to pack the crates containing the amber panels into trucks and drove the treasure away to safety. Koch was later captured by the Allies, and in 1965 when being questioned by Polish authorities apparently revealed that the Amber Room had been sealed inside a bunker on the outskirts of Königsberg. The location of this bunker had apparently been lost due to the destruction caused by the bombing in the area. However, this is contradicted by Rohde, who stated that the boxes were still in the castle as late as April 5, 1945.

The German military commander of Königsberg, General Otto Lasch, finally surrendered the town on April 9, 1945, and the Red Army took over. After this the Amber Room was never seen in public again, but what had happened to it?

Shortly after the capture of Königsberg the Council of People's Commissars sent professor Alexander Ivanovich Brusov of the State Historical Museum in Moscow to the city to investigate the fate of the Amber Room. When Brusov and his team entered the Knights' Hall all they found were the charred fragments of the once-great treasure, which had apparently been completely destroyed by a devastating fire. He wrote in June 1945 that his investigations had revealed that "the Amber Room was destroyed between 9 and 11 April 1945"[2] — in other words, during the final days of the Battle of Königsberg, which finished on April 9th. Brusov also located a witness, Paul Feyerabend, manager of the Blood Court restaurant, located underneath the Knights' Hall, and someone who had been in the castle when it was captured by the Red Army. Feyerabend stated that the crates containing the Amber Room had never been evacuated from the building but had perished in the flames that devastated the northern wing of the building.

That the Amber Room was destroyed during the battle or shortly afterward by the Red Army as they rampaged through the city is the most prosaic explanation of its fate. This was the conclusion arrived at by English investigative journalists Catherine Scott-Clark and Adrian Levy, after they had undertaken detailed research for their 2004 book on the subject, *The Amber Room: The Fate of the World's Greatest Lost Treasure.* Unsurprisingly, not everyone agrees with this conclusion, and Scott-Clark and Levy's book aroused much anger at the time of its publication from Russian officials who claimed that the authors' hypothesis was completely untrue. Retired General Valentin Varennikov, deputy head of the Soviet General Staff from 1979 to 1984, called the book "propagandist claptrap," and former Russian Minister of Culture Mikhail Shvydkoi accused the authors of "revising history."[3] Probably the first to dispute the theory that the Amber Room had perished in the flames at Königsberg castle was Anatoly Mikhailovich Kuchumov, the curator of the Tsarskoye Selo museum we met earlier.

In March 1946 the Council of People's Commissars decided to send Kuchumov to Königsberg on a top-secret mission to investigate whether the Amber Room had indeed been destroyed, as Brusov had maintained. On arrival at the castle, Kuchumov found that only the corner of the castle containing the Knights' Hall remained standing. After searching through the ruins Kuchumov discovered underneath layers of ash "three stone mosaic pictures...that once decorated the Amber Room" and stated that the items were "totally burned and discoloured."[4] Kuchumov also apparently discovered a hoard of fire-damaged German letters that revealed that the Nazis had planned to get the Amber Room out when Allied bombing in the area began in August 1944. One of these letters, dated January 12, 1945, reported that the Amber Room was being packed ready for transport to safety in a castle in western Saxony (a historical region of eastern Germany). However, as all rail, air, and sea routes out of Königsberg were being cut off by the Allies (there were no trains out after January 22nd), could the Germans have got the heavy crates containing the pieces of the Amber Room out in time?

One theory about how the Amber Room was evacuated is that it was loaded aboard the huge Nazi cruise ship the *M.S. Wilhelm Gustloff*, which left port at Gotenhafen (modern Gdynia, in the north of modern Poland) on January 30, 1945. The *Wilhelm Gustloff*, which was being used as an escape ship by the Germans, was sunk later that day by a Soviet submarine with the tragic loss of an incredible 9,500 lives, the largest loss of life from a shipwreck in maritime history. The wreck of the *Wilhelm Gustloff* has been visited several times throughout the years by divers in search of the lost treasure, but no trace has ever been found. The question one has to ask is this: Would the Nazis have risked transporting something as valuable as the Amber Room on a ship full to overflowing and heading out into the hazards of the Baltic Sea and Soviet submarines?

In December 1949, Kuchumov was sent back to Königsberg (by then renamed Kaliningrad), to begin another government-sponsored, top-secret search for the Amber Room, under the pretense that he and his team were searching for oil. With various conflicting tales circulating that the boxes containing the amber panels had been hidden in a sealed subterranean bunker in Königsberg, buried in mines in the Ore Mountains (on the border between the Czech Republic and the federal German state of Saxony), or even smuggled out to America, Kuchumov had his work cut out in finding any trace of the treasured room. And indeed, after a 10-year search Kuchumov and his team had nothing to show for their work. Perhaps a new approach was needed. On July 6, 1958, Soviet newspaper *Kaliningradskaya Pravda* published a story entitled "The Search Continues for the Missing Amber Room," the first of a series of three articles about the Soviet search for the Room, which was apparently no longer considered top secret. In these stories a journalist named Vladimir Dmetriev called for help from the public in locating the lost treasure and loudly proclaimed that the investigations of Professor Brusov in Königsberg in 1945 were unprofessional and error-ridden and his conclusions about the fate of the Amber Room consequently untrustworthy.

However, in their investigations for their book about the Amber Room, Catherine Scott-Clark and Adrian Levy carried out extensive research into Vladimir Dmetriev and found no trace of his name in journalistic databases or at *Kaliningradskaya Pravda*. Their conclusion is that "Vladimir Dmetriev" was probably a pseudonym, most likely for Anatoly Mikhailovich Kuchumov.[5] Nevertheless the sensational article in *Kaliningradskaya Pravda* had the desired effect, and within a couple of days it was being carried by other newspapers, as well as East German magazine *Freie Welt,* which brought the story to a huge audience in the eastern bloc countries.

As a result of these articles, Amber Room fever spread across central and Eastern Europe. Thousands of replies poured in to answer the plea for information from the pen of "Vladimir Dmetriev." These replies came from art historians, former Red Army soldiers, high-ranking officials, civilians, and amateur treasure hunters, some of whom believed they had important information about the Amber Room. The Soviet Union even convinced East

Germany of the possibility of recovering the Amber Room, and indeed, the files of the Stasi, the East German state security service, contain 180,000 pages related to the Amber Room. However, despite decades of expensive investigations into the lost treasure, the Stasi, like their counterparts in the Soviet Union, turned up nothing. Catherine Scott-Clark and Adrian Levy point out that during the Stasi's 26 years of investigation into the Amber Room, not once did the KGB agree to share any intelligence on the subject with the East Germans.[6]

In 1967 the Soviet government founded a Special Commission to search for the Amber Room, but despite their extensive research and explorations of numerous alleged hiding places for the room, nothing of note was discovered, and the Commission was dissolved in 1984. The organization of these numerous unsuccessful searches by Soviet authorities over the last 60 years or so begs the question of what their motives were. Were the Soviets utilizing the theft and possible destruction of the Amber Room by the Germans as a propaganda tool? Or is it possible that the Soviets were covering their own tracks, preserving the myth of the survival of the great lost treasure, having realized early on that it was perhaps its own Red Army who had inadvertently destroyed the Amber Room during the siege of Königsberg early in 1945? The truth of the latter explanation is indicated by Soviet refusal to share information on their search for the Amber Room with the East Germans and the fact that back in April of 1946 Kuchumov had also interrogated Paul Feyerabend, and Feyerabend had given him the same version of events as he gave Brusov, though Kuchumov chose to ignore him. Perhaps Kuchumov's guilt about not acting quickly enough to save the Amber Room from the Germans in 1941 was beginning to affect his actions.

The apparent loss of the Amber Room to fire in 1945 has not convinced everyone that there is nothing left to search for. Apart from the Soviet government and the Stasi, hundreds of groups and individuals have organized extensive searches for the treasure in mines, lagoons, and hidden bunkers throughout Europe, all without success. Various alternative and conflicting theories as to the location of the Amber Room, some more believable than others, have also emerged over the years. These range from the relatively sane theory that the panels, or some of them, survived intact and are still hidden in a bunker in Kaliningrad, to perhaps the most extreme: that Stalin had a second Amber Room built and it was this fake room that the Germans actually stole in 1941. Some researchers believe that the Amber Room survives and is currently in the collection of a shadowy antiquities collector or group with connections either to the Soviet military or to a Nazi cabal of some kind.

In February 2008 it was sensationally reported that the long search for the Amber Room was finally over when a group of German treasure hunters claimed to have located it along with two tons of Nazi gold in an abandoned copper mine in the Ore Mountains. Spokesman for the group Heinz-Peter Haustein, the mayor of the nearby village of Deutschneudorf, had been on the trail of the Amber Room for a decade in the region and stated to *Spiegel Online* that he was more than 90% sure that he had at last discovered the lost Prussian treasure.[7] Haustein told *Spiegal Online* that the chamber his team had located using electromagnetic pulse measurements was probably "part of a labyrinth of storage rooms that the Nazis built here" and that a friend had told him before he died that "the Nazis sent truckloads and trainloads of valuables to this area throughout the spring of 1945."[8] However, since these bold statements were made, nothing has been heard of Haustein and his fantastic discovery.

A number of researchers believe that, though much of the Amber Room was indeed burnt in the fire at Königsberg castle, some pieces survived but were looted by Russian or German soldiers, and subsequently became scattered throughout the world. A crucial piece of evidence seemingly in favor of this latter theory came to light in Bremen, northwest Germany, in 1997. A German pensioner named Hans Achtermann was arrested in the city after his lawyer was caught trying to sell one of the four jeweled Florentine mosaic panels from the Amber Room to an antiquities dealer for $2.5 million. It later emerged that Achtermann was the son of a German officer who had been part of the convoy that brought the amber panels to Königsberg in 1941, though Achtermann claimed he did not know how his father obtained the mosaic. It was thought that Achtermann's father may have taken the panel as the convoy was bombed on its way to Königsberg, though there is no reason why he then couldn't have returned the object when he reached the city. It is perhaps more likely that the officer purloined the treasure during the chaotic evacuation of Königsberg in 1945, when perhaps one missing panel would be less likely to be noticed amid the general panic.

Whatever happened during WWII, in 1997 the German government ordered Hans Achtermann to hand over the treasure. When he refused, with the prospect of a lengthy legal battle ahead, a local businessman stepped in and reportedly paid $100,000 to Achtermann and his family not to sue to reclaim the panel. A few weeks after the sensational discovery of the panel an ornately inlaid chest of drawers from the Amber Room turned up in Berlin. An unnamed woman had purchased the chest from Stasi art dealers in the 1970s, but had recognized it in a TV report about the Amber Room and turned it over to German authorities. In 2000, officials from Berlin handed over the recovered panel and the chest to Russian President Vladimir Putin in exchange for 101 drawings that had been taken from Karnzow Castle, Brandenburg, by the Red Army in 1945. These masterpieces were part of the Baldin Collection, a group of 364 drawings and paintings looted from Germany and taken to the Soviet Union by a Soviet army captain named Viktor Baldin during WWII.

It is common for most treasure hunting stories to have a curse that affects those involved in discovering or searching for the treasure, and the Amber Room is no exception. It is true that there are one or two suspicious deaths connected with the treasure, beginning with Dr. Alfred Rohde and his wife, who both died in Königsberg in December 1945 during the typhoid epidemic that swept through the city. Their deaths apparently occurred the day before they were to be interrogated by the NKVD (the People's Commissariat for Internal Affairs) during Soviet investigations into the fate of the Amber Room. Another alleged victim was Yuri Gusev, deputy head of the Main Intelligence Department of Russia's foreign military intelligence unit, the GRU, who died in a mysterious car crash in Moscow in November 1992. Gusev's colleagues at the GRU later established that he had, in fact, been murdered. At the time Gusev had allegedly been giving information to a journalist investigating the whereabouts of the Amber Room, though there seems to be no direct evidence of this.

Something that perhaps shines some light on Gusev's death is that in August 2010 the body of Major-General Yuri Ivanov, another deputy head of the GNU, washed up on a Turkish beach after he had disappeared while on holiday in Syria. The Kremlin stated that Ivanov had died in a tragic swimming accident, though it was suggested by some media sources that he had been on official business and had in the past been employed reviewing military installations in Syria. What is a little suspicious is that the Syrian resort Ivanov was staying at, Latakia, is located relatively close to a strategically important Russian naval facility at the port of Tartus. More directly connected to the intrigues of the Amber Room is the death in 1987 of ex-soldier, strawberry farmer, and treasure hunter Georg Stein, who was found naked in a forest near Munich with two kitchen knives in his stomach. Apparently Stein had discovered a radio message giving details of the concealment of the Amber Room after it had supposedly been destroyed, though again there is no physical proof of this.

On May 31, 2003, 40 heads of state arrived in St. Petersburg to attend celebrations to mark the 300th anniversary of the city. The centerpiece of these celebrations was the unveiling of a reconstruction of the Amber Room, a painstaking and hugely expensive work 20 years in the making. Modern Russian craftsmen used six tons of amber in the reconstruction of the lost treasure and based their work on surviving fragments of the room (including the panel discovered in Bremen in 1997), old black and white photographs, and one color slide. The new Amber Room was dedicated by Russian President Vladimir Putin and German Chancellor Gerhard Schröder, and is now on display at the partially restored Catherine Palace. As to the fate of the original Amber Room, available evidence does indicate that the majority of it perished in the flames at Königsberg castle in 1945. However, the discovery in Bremen in 1997 suggests that there may be other pieces out there, perhaps smuggled out of Germany in the chaos that followed the Battle of Königsberg, but whether these remnants survive intact as recognizable pieces of the 300-year-old Prussian treasure is another matter.

*Fake Ancient Treasures*

This chapter deals with a number of fake ancient treasures that have surfaced over the years, some of which have managed to fool art experts for decades before being discovered. As the four examples I have chosen show, fake treasures have many of the characteristics of real ones: the generally high quality of the craftsmanship, the uncertain provenance, a shady history of ownership, and the huge market values placed on the items when they come into the public eye.

In terms of the wider field of archaeological forgeries, a few well-known examples will suffice. The pieces of a skull and a jawbone of an alleged early hominid found in Piltdown, East Sussex, England, in 1912 were thought for years to represent the remains of a previously unknown early human. It was not until 1953 that the hoax of the Piltdown Man was exposed and the specimen revealed to be the skull of a man combined with the lower jawbone of an orangutan. The majority of the infamous "Crystal Skulls," supposedly ancient American artifacts made of rock crystal, were found to have been made in Europe in the 19th century, though this fact has not affected some people's beliefs in the mystical powers of these objects. The Etruscan Terracotta Warriors, bought by the Metropolitan Museum of Art in New York between 1915 and 1921, were eventually shown up as fakes in 1960, when they were traced to the Ricardis, a family of Italian art forgers. The James Ossuary, a limestone coffin discovered in Israel in 2002, was believed to be the ossuary of Jesus' brother James because of the Aramaic inscription engraved on one of its sides. However, scholars examining the inscription found it to be fake, and tests showed that the patina applied to make the inscription look old was, in fact, modern.

The reasons why these fakes are made and why so many people are taken in by them are as varied as the range of fake artifacts themselves. But often, as in the cases of the Etruscan Terracotta Warriors and the Crystal Skulls, the fakes are manufactured to sell and make a lot of money; it is as simple as that. This is also the case with the James Ossuary and with the many other fake biblical artifacts, like the Jehoash Inscription, for example. But many people are also taken in by fake biblical artifacts because they support their religious beliefs and are important tools in helping to prove the "truth" of the Bible. The Piltdown Man, on the other hand, may merely have been a practical joke that got out of hand, but it embarrassed many of the scientists of the day who believed the skull was the "missing link" between apes and humans. Preconceived beliefs, whether religious or otherwise, can often lead to the unquestioning acceptance of artifacts which appear to support that belief.

The problem of fake archaeological artifacts is not a new one, but it is becoming increasingly common as counterfeit ancient coins, jewelry, statues, weapons, and even mummies flood the marketplace and pollute the archaeological record. From sales on eBay for a few hundred dollars to million-dollar deals with some of the world's biggest museums, archaeological forgery is a thriving business. Such fakes will continue to be manufactured and sold, often on the black market, as long as people are willing to buy artifacts without a secure provenance from dishonest antiquities dealers and private individuals whose only motivation is profit.

## ~Saitaphernes's Golden Tiara

The Scythians were a nomadic people of Iranian origin who inhabited the vast area of steppeland from what is now the Crimea, east of the Aral Sea in present-day Uzbekistan and Kazakhstan (once part of the former Soviet Union), from around the eighth century BC until the fourth century BC. The Scythians were renowned for their horsemanship and knowledge of horses, as well as for burying their dead in huge burial mounds known as *kurgans*. These kurgans have provided archaeologists with a wealth of artifacts that provide us with vital knowledge about the Scythians and their way of life, as well as their beliefs about death and the afterlife. Such burial goods include gold drinking cups, beautifully worked gold and silver jewelry, gold animal figures, bronze helmets and arrowheads, and iron swords sometimes with highly decorated gold-covered scabbards.

In the 19th century investigations of Scythian kurgans and their often-rich treasures resulted in a huge market for Scythian gold artifacts, and museums and individual collectors throughout Europe were on the lookout for more treasure from this area of the world. In 1830, at the site of Kul Oba, near Kerch in eastern Crimea (modern-day Ukraine), the stone burial vault of a Scythian king, his wife, and servant was discovered inside a kurgan. The fourth-century BC tomb contained an exquisite collection of grave goods, including a gold torque, a pair of gold pendant discs showing the head of the Greek goddess Athena, a gold bracelet ending in two sphinxes, and a unique round-sided goblet made of electrum and illustrated with Scythian male figures. Another incredible collection of Scythian objects, including a gold cover plate of a quiver showing scenes from the life of Achilles, a gold plaque in the form of the head of Dionysus, and an exquisite silver amphora with relief decoration of Scythians taming horses, came from the fourth-century BC Chertomlyk kurgan, northwest of the city of Nikopol (modern Ukraine), and was excavated in 1863. The majority of the finds from these kurgans eventually found their way to the State Hermitage Museum in St. Petersburg.

*17.1. The "Saitaphernes tiara." Photo from* La Nature *journal, 1896. Courtesy of Wikipedia.*

In 1895 a story appeared in a Vienna newspaper about peasants in Crimea making an extraordinary find but having to escape Russia in fear their discovery would be seized by the authorities. In Vienna in February 1896, a Russian grain merchant and part-time art dealer from Ochakov (now in the Ukraine), Schapschelle Hochmann, and his brother exhibited a collection of ancient gold jewelry and other gold work. The collection included an extraordinary tiara, which Hochmann said was found among the ruins of the former ancient Greek colony at Olbia on the Black Sea, near Odessa. The oval-shaped gold tiara was about 7 inches in height, and weighed just more than a pound. Its beautiful decoration was divided into bands, the lower of which showed scenes from Scythian life, while the upper band illustrated episodes from the *Iliad,* including the quarrel between Agamemnon and Achilles over the captive princess Briseis. An inscription in Greek on the object stated that the tiara was a gift from "The Senate and People of Olbia to the Great Invincible Saitaphernes." Saitaphernes was apparently a third-century BC Scythian king.

Hochmann attempted to sell his collection through Vienna agents Szymanski and Anton Vogel, to Vienna's Imperial Court Museum, but although a number of collector's who viewed the objects were convinced they were genuine, the museum's director, Bruno Buchner, expressed severe doubts and declined to purchase them. The British Museum had also been offered the treasure by letter, but it, too, turned down the opportunity. In March 1896, Vogel and Szymanski took the objects to Paris to try to interest the Louvre in purchasing them. Two experts on ancient art, M.A. Kaempfen, director of the National Museums and of the Louvre, and M.E. Hron de Villefosse, keeper of the Greco-Roman Department of the Louvre, were called in to closely examine the artifacts. They both found the objects to be genuine and recommended that the Louvre purchase the tiara without hesitation, which it did soon after, along with an "antique" gold necklace and pendant, for the sum of 200,000 gold French francs (about $40,000). On April 1, 1896, the Louvre proudly put the Tiara of Saitaphernes (as it was now known) on display in its Antiquities Department. But soon questions began to be asked as to its origin.

The first to voice his doubts was Munich archaeologist Adolf Furtwangler, who commented on inconsistencies in the style and design of the tiara, as well as the apparent lack of aging on the object. Soon he would denounce the tiara as a poorly made forgery. Other experts, including a Professor Vesselovsky of the

University of St. Petersburg, who believed the object a typical example of the modern forgeries coming from the Hochmanns' shop in Ochakov, also expressed their serious doubts about the tiara. Despite the objections and much debate in the press, the Louvre stood firm in its belief that the object was genuine.

On March 11, 1903, a Montmartre artist who went under the name Rodolphe Elina (real name Henry Mayence) was charged with forging paintings by artist Henri Pilles. Mayence then sensationally claimed that he had also made the Tiara of Saitaphernes, a statement that soon hit the headlines all over the world. On March 23rd, newspaper *Le Matin* published a letter written by a resident of Paris, a Russian jeweler named Lifschiu. He stated that he had watched a close friend of his, a highly skilled goldsmith named Israel Ruchomovsky, work on the tiara, and that it had taken him eight months to complete the task in 1895–96, for which he was paid 2,000 rubles. When contacted in Odessa, Ruchomovsky stated that he had indeed produced the tiara and that it had been made for a person from Kertsch (now in eastern Crimea). To prove his assertion, Ruchomovsky traveled to Paris and informed the officials at the Louvre that he had been commissioned to make the tiara by the two Hochmann brothers, as a gift to a Russian archaeologist, but that they had not told him the true purpose of the tiara. When Ruchomovsky was to begin work on the artifact, Hochmann had sent him illustrated books to help him, one of which was *Antiquités de la Russsie Méridionale* (*Antiquities of South Russia*), published in 1891 and written by Tolstoy-Kondekof-Reinach. Another was the *Bilder-Atlas zur Weltgeschichte* (*Picture Atlas of World History*) by Ludwig Weisser, published in 1860.

Ruchomovsky also described how he made the tiara in three separate sections, which he had then soldered together, and explained precisely how he had faked the signs of damage and age. On examination of the tiara, the goldsmith's statements were found to be accurate, but the Louvre still required conclusive proof that their prized object was a fake. So at the request of an independent parliamentary committee, Ruchomovsky was asked to reconstruct a part of the tiara in gold without the use of the original object as reference. Ruchomovsky completed the task and in doing so practically sealed the fate of the Tiara of Saitaphernes as a modern forgery. Hugely embarrassed at how easily their experts had been fooled, the Louvre removed the tiara from display and put it into storage. However, the tiara did see the light of day again in 1954 as part of the Louvre's "Salon of Fakes" exhibit, and in 1997 it went out on loan to the Israel Museum in Jerusalem, which was staging an exhibition about Ruchomovksy.

Meanwhile, the talents of the poor goldsmith from Odessa had aroused much interest in Paris, and Ruchomovsky was soon inundated with orders from French jewelers. He exhibited his work at the Paris Salon of decorative arts from 1904 to 1906, and was soon able to bring his family from Odessa to Paris, where he remained until his death in 1934. On November 24, 1998, Christies in Amsterdam auctioned an exquisite miniature gold human skeleton and silver gilt sarcophagus that had been crafted by Ruchomovsky between 1892 and 1901 in Odessa and that he had signed in several places. The estimate for the 3 1/2-inch-long item was $103,902–$155,852, though it was finally sold for an incredible $311,530. Perhaps Ruchomovsky would be amused that it is the Louvre that has been left with a rather different skeleton in its closet.

### ≈ The Persian Princess

In November 2000, the international press announced the discovery of an ornately adorned 2,600-year-old female mummy in Pakistan. Dubbed the "Persian Princess," the mummy wore a gold crown and face mask, and had a gold breastplate placed over her crossed arms bearing a cuneiform inscription identifying her as the daughter of renowned Persian king Xerxes I (519 BC–465 BC). The mummy had apparently been offered for sale on the antiquities black market for $50 million. However, after much publicity and lengthy investigations, doubts were cast on both the age of the mummy and its provenance. The most chilling conclusion of the examination of the princess mummy linked it to a brutal murder and a deeply disturbing side of international antiquity trafficking.

In mid-October 2001 Pakistani authorities received information about an Iranian resident of Karachi named Ali Aqbar, who had made a videotape of an ancient mummy he was trying to sell. After his arrest and interrogation Aqbar led the police to the house of local tribal chieftain, Sardar Wali Reeki, in the town of Quetta, in the southwestern province of Balochistan, near the Pakistani border with Afghanistan. Aqbar also told the police that Sardar Wali Reeki had other valuable artifacts stored in his house, suggesting that he was involved in the illegal antiquities trade. When the house was raided the police located the mummy, which Reeki claimed he had obtained from an Iranian named Sharif Shah Bakhi, who had discovered it some years before in the Kharan district of Balochistan province after an earthquake. Reeki admitted that he had been trying to sell the item on the antiquities black market for $50 million, but so far had only been offered $1.1 million. Both Reeki and Akbar were charged under Pakistan's Antiquity Act, which carries a 10-year maximum jail sentence. However the supposed discoverer of the mummy, Sharif Shah Bakhi, was never found.

Despite the questionable circumstances surroundings the discovery, the mummy princess was an astounding find and was immediately taken to Pakistan's National Museum in Karachi. The news of the Persian Princess spread quickly and at a preliminary press conference on October 26th, professor Ahmad Hasan Dani, an archaeologist at Islamabad's Quaid-e-Azam University, stated that as mummies were not found in Pakistan or Iran it must have come from outside, probably from Egypt. Noting the fact that the mummy was wrapped in bandages in the Egyptian style, though the cuneiform inscription on the plate was in Persian, Hasan Dani suggested that she may have been an Egyptian princess who married a Persian prince.

Further examination of the mummy revealed that she had been placed on top of a layer of wax and honey, and was contained inside a stone coffin set in an elaborately carved wooden sar-cophagus. The sarcophagus was decorated with an engraving of Ahura Mazda, the supreme Zoroastrian deity, as well as other Persian symbols associated with Xerxes. Initial examination of the mummy suggested that her name was Khor-ul-Gayan or Tundal Gayan, an 18-year-old Persian princess, possibly the daughter of Karoosh-ul-Kabir, the first ruler of Persia's Khamam-ul-Nishiyan Dynasty, which was established around 600 BC. But the transla-tion of the inscription on her breastplate was much more sen-sational, reading "I am the daughter of the great King Xerxes. Mazereka protect me. I am Rhodugune, I am." Could the mummy be a little-known daughter of the great Persian king? Asma Ibra-him, the curator of the National Museum in Karachi, where the mummy was kept and examined, suggested the mummy may have been looted from a tomb in the Hamadan region of western Iran, though she was aware that there was no evidence that the Persians mummified their dead in the way the Egyptians did.

As more investigations were carried out into the Persian mummy a dispute broke out between Iran and Pakistan, not the most amiable of neighbors to begin with, about who owned the mummy. The Iranian Cultural Heritage Organization claimed that, as the mummy was a member of the Persian royal fam-ily, she should be returned to the land of her origin. Pakistan, meanwhile, stated that as she had been found in Balochistan she should remain where she was. Even the Taliban got in on the act, claiming she had in fact been discovered over the border in Afghanistan and therefore in its territory.

There was yet another strand to the already-complex story of the Persian mummy. In March 2001, Oscar White Muscarella, former curator at the Metropolitan Museum of Art in New York and a specialist in the antique art and archaeology of the Near East, received four Polaroid photographs of a mummy in a wooden coffin. The sender of the photos was a New Jersey res-ident named Amanollah Riggi, who was acting on behalf of an anonymous antiquities dealer in Pakistan. Riggi also supplied Muscarella with a translation of a cuneiform inscription visible in the photos on the mummy's gold breastplate. The inscription, Riggi informed Muscarella, which had been translated by a "cuneiform expert at a major American university,"[1] stated that the mummy was the daughter of the fifth-century BC Persian King Xerxes. Riggi also said that the owners had a video showing the mummy that could be sent to New York if the Met was interested in purchasing the item.

Suspecting all was not right with the mummy and the inscription, Muscarella contacted the cuneiform expert who had translated the inscription and found out that, although the text did identify the mummy as the daughter of Xerxes, there had been another page of the analysis that Riggi had not shown him. This second part of the report identified various inconsistencies in the supposedly Old Persian text, which led the expert to doubt the genuineness of the inscription. Muscarella also had his own doubts about the authenticity of some of the carvings on the wooden coffin and decided to have nothing more to do with Riggi. But seven months later when Muscarella heard about the newly discovered Persian Princess, he knew that it must be the same mummy he had been shown photos of in March 2001. Through the U.S. publication *Archaeology* Magazine Muscarella's findings about the mummy were sent on to the FBI, who passed them on to Interpol.

At the National Museum of Pakistan, Asma Ibrahim was carrying out a detailed examination of the Persian mummy. One of the first things she noticed while scrutinizing the text on the breastplate was that the name "Rhodugune" was in fact the later Greek version of the princess's original Persian name, "Wardegauna." Ibrahim was puzzled and could think of no logical explanation for the Persians using the Greek version of the princess's name. Further examination revealed more textual mistakes in the inscription, and when Ibrahim discovered lead pencil marks on the coffin, which had obviously been made to guide the carvings, she became doubtful of the supposed ancient origin of the princess. The mummy was subsequently sent to the Agha Khan University Hospital for CAT and X-ray scans to determine more about its origins. These tests revealed that the organs had been removed from the body, as was normal in the ancient Egyptian mummification process, and the cavities filled with powder (which later proved to be baking soda and salt). However, the heart had also been removed, a practice unknown in ancient Egypt. The tests also showed that the woman's back was broken and, inexplicably if the body was ancient, some of her tendons and ligaments were still intact.

Now convinced the mummy had to be a fake, Ibrahim sent samples of the wooden coffin, the reed matting on which the mummy lay, the bandages, and resins off to the German Archaeological Institute in Berlin for radio carbon analysis. The results confirmed Ibrahim's suspicions: The reed mat had only been made in the last 50 years. Furthermore, radiocarbon dating of the corpse itself, also carried out in Germany, revealed a date for the mummy of between 1994 and 1996. Ibrahim published her findings in an 11-page report on April 17, 2001. Her conclusions were that the so-called "Persian Princess" was in fact a modern woman, about 21–25 years old, who had died around 1996, possibly killed with a blunt instrument to the back of the head. Sometime later, further analysis of the mummy revealed that the bones showed signs of osteoporosis, indicating she was in fact a middle-aged woman, perhaps around 50 years old, who had dyed blonde hair, and who had suffered both a broken neck and a broken spine, either of which could have caused her death. Although it was not possible to tell if her injuries were the result of an accident or something more disturbing, the police opened a murder inquiry and apparently arrested a number of suspects in Balochistan. The woman's face was reconstructed using computer software and revealed to be characteristic of inhabitants of the border region of Pakistan and Iran, though her identity was never traced, and nothing came of the murder inquiry.

The implications of Ibrahim's findings are indeed sinister. The whole process of creating a fake mummy that could fool experts even for a few days would have required a team of people skilled in many different areas, including ancient art, archaeology, and anatomy, not to mention the facilities in which to carry out the forgery, as well as the various chemicals and other materials needed in the manufacture. If the woman's body had been taken from a grave, then it would need to have been done soon after burial, because in hot countries such as Pakistan and Iran bodies decompose quickly. However, the forger's desperate need for a fresh body and the violence of the woman's injuries indicate she may well have been murdered. Either way, it is a shocking act. Disturbingly, at least two more "Persian mummies" have appeared for sale in recent years on the antiquities black market, possibly indicating other victims in this murderous trade. One also wonders how many of these macabre fakes have already been sold to unsuspecting collectors who chose not to have them properly authenticated.

### ∽The Chiemsee Cauldron

In May 2001 a local amateur diver discovered a strange gold cup while diving in Lake Chiemsee, a tourist destination east of the city of Rosenheim, Bavaria, Germany. The object had been lying in the mud on the bottom of the lake about 655 feet from the northern shore, near Seebruck. The diver took the object to an art dealer known only as Thorsten K and in late 2001/early 2002 the pair sent the cup to Dr. Ludwig Wamser, head of the Bavarian State Archaeological Collection in Munich, for analysis. An initial inspection revealed that the cup was made of 18-carat gold, measured 20 inches in diameter and 12 inches in height, and weighed 23 pounds. But it was the decoration on the cup that caught the archaeologist's attention. The repoussé (raised in relief) decoration, illustrating heavily stylized mythical Celtic symbols, horned deities, fantastic animals, and hunters wielding huge trumpets, drew parallels with a mysterious ancient artifact known as the Gundestrup Cauldron.

The Gundestrup cauldron is a lavishly decorated silver vessel, dating between the second and first centuries BC, placing it within the late La Tène (European Iron Age) culture or early Roman Iron Age. The vessel, which measures 27 inches in diameter and 16.5

inches in height, and weighs about 20 pounds, was discovered in a small peat bog at Gundestrup, in the Aars parish of Himmerland, Denmark, on May 28, 1891. The incredible vessel is made up of 13 panels decorated with repoussé portrayals of deities, fabulous creatures, wheel symbols, warriors, trumpeteers, and ritual scenes, which have been associated with various aspects of Iron Age Celtic religion, though its exact origins and purpose remain elusive. Could the Chiemsee Cauldron be in some way related to the 2,000-year-old example from Gundestrup? At first Dr. Wamser thought it was, and in February 2002 gave a presentation in Würzburg University's Toscana Hall, lauding what was now the "Chiemsee Cauldron" as the "Celtic discovery of the century."

*17.2. Lake Chiemsee. Courtesy of Wikipedia.*

There was speculation that the gold cup had been an ancient ritual deposit in Lake Chiemsee, and researchers noted that Iron Age Celtic finds, including coins, had been found in the area around the lake. There was apparently another similarity between the Chiemsee Cauldron and the Gundestrup Cauldron: They were both found in water, and therefore could have been votive deposits to Celtic deities, perhaps akin to the Llyn Cerrig Bach hoard of bronze and iron objects deposited in a lake in the northwest of the island of Anglesey, Wales, from about 300 BC to AD 100. However, although the Gundestrup Cauldron had been found in a bog, when it was originally deposited 2,000 or so years ago the area had in fact been dry land, so the object had either been lost or thrown away, and was possibly connected to the defended Iron Age settlement that lies nearby, rather than being a ritual deposit.

However, unbeknown to his audience at Toscana Hall, Dr. Wamser had carried out a close examination of the Chiemsee Cauldron and discovered that although the artistic style was indeed Iron Age Celtic in appearance, the metal had in fact been soldered, which put its date firmly in the 20th century. So after initially building up the importance of the cauldron, Dr. Wamser announced to the stunned lecture audience that the gold cauldron was a fake, probably constructed in the 1930s by the Nazis, who he said had planned to build a huge education center on the shore of Lake Chiemsee to spread their ideology. When this plan was thwarted, the object may have been thrown into the lake to avoid it falling into the hands of advancing U.S. troops. This theory was supported by a claim made by a man named Theodor Heiden, who stated that his jeweler's company's goldsmith, Alfred Notz, had told him some time before his death in the 1960s about a "golden cauldron weighing more than 10 kilograms (22 lbs.), with a figurative ornament and manufactured by means of the paddle and anvil technique."[2] Apparently the cauldron had been manufactured in Heiden's Munich workshop between 1925 and 1939, at the request of the company Elektrochemische Werke München in Hollriegelskreuth, just to the south of Munich. The director of this company, Nazi supporter Albert Pietzsch, also head of the Reich Chamber of Commerce and an associate of Hitler, is supposed to have been a customer of the goldsmith's workshop. Had the Nazis manufactured an expensive copy of the Gundestrup cauldron because of what they interpreted as its Germanic imagery?

Whatever the truth of this story, when news of the Chiemsee Cauldron broke in early August 2002, despite the fact that it was a 20th-century creation, its gold value alone was worth an estimated $96,000. Rumors also began to spread of the existence of lost Nazi gold that had been sunk in Lake Chiemsee at the end of

WWII, and that the gold cup had been a kind of Nazi Holy Grail, which had been used in occult initiation rites in Herrenchiemsee castle, located on an island in the lake. But such speculation was forced into the background when it came to the issue of the ownership and possible sale of the Chiemsee Cauldron. Bernd Schreiber, Bavarian Finance Ministry spokesman, said that if it was established that the cup was the property of the Nazis then the diver who discovered the object would receive nothing, as such items are considered the property of the state. However, proof that the Chiemsee Cauldron was manufactured by the Nazis was never found, and an agreement was reached between the Bavarian state and the finder to share the proceeds of the object's sale in 2003 for a reputed 300,000 Euro (about $390,000 at current exchange rates) to a Munich businessman. This price represented almost twice the market value of the gold in the cup.

In 2005 the cauldron was re-sold to a former CEO of a large Swiss distributor in Zurich. The new owner of the Chiemsee Cauldron, known only as "Martin K," lost no time in trying to attract investors to what he claimed was an incredibly significant ancient artifact "probably the most important art-historical discovery in the Western Hemisphere."[3] According to Martin K, the object's value had also risen significantly: "experts believe its value could reach a sum of around €1 billion"[4] ($1.4 billion). Soon he was marketing the cauldron as the original Holy Grail, and had attracted investors from Kazakhstan who transferred €1.1 million ($1.5 million) to his Swiss account via a Moscow bank; others apparently followed, and soon the Swiss businessman had received 7.4 million Euros in investments.

But as time went on it was clear that the sale of the Chiemsee Cauldron was not likely to happen, and the investors grew suspicious. In March 2006 they reported the matter to the authorities. Charges were files against the Swiss businessman, who was later revealed to be Marcel Wunderli, director of Morgan Stanwick Ltd., a private limited company located in the Canton of St. Gallen, in northeast Switzerland, who were involved in the "management of and trade in art and antiquities."[5] In 2007 the cauldron was confiscated by Swiss authorities, and on October 27, 2010, a fraud trial began against Wunderli. Meanwhile, Morgan Stanwick Ltd. was dissolved, leaving behind millions of dollars in claims. In August 2012, 63-year-old Wunderli was given a three-year jail sentence for fraud by a Zurich court. The result of these proceedings is that the Chiemsee Cauldron, whatever its origin, is in legal limbo, hidden away in a vault of the Zurich Cantonal Bank as part of the bankrupt company's estate.

## ⋍A Nazi Buddha From Space

The 1938–1939 German Expedition to Tibet led by German zoologist Ernst Schäfer has often been associated in popular culture with a Nazi occult mission to discover a secret subterranean realm and make contact with the Nazi's Aryan forefathers hidden in the Himalayas. Books like Pauwels and Bergier's *The Morning of the Magicians* (1960) and Trevor Ravenscroft's *The Spear of Destiny* (1973) make these claims, although there is no hard evidence to back them up. The real purpose of the German expedition of 1938–1939 was more mundane: to create a complete scientific record of Tibet and bring back important zoological and botanical samples. It was apparently during this expedition that Schäfer discovered a strange statue and brought it back to Germany.

The stone statue of a bearded figure wearing trousers, which measures 9.4 inches in height and weighs 22 pounds, is thought to depict the Buddhist god Vaisravana. The figure has an earring in his right ear, bears a Buddhist swastika on his armoured breastplate, and is holding a round object in his left hand. Could the swastika symbol on the statue have been the motivation for its theft from Tibet? The Buddha statue seemingly disappeared during WWII, after which it changed hands between various private collectors until it came up for auction in 2007, and its new Munich-based owner decided to have it scientifically tested in Germany. Researchers dated the unique statue stylistically to the 11th century AD. But it was the scientific tests that were to prove most astonishing. After chemical analyses of the object, Dr. Elmar Buchner, of the Institute for Planetary Sciences at the University of Stuttgart, stated that the concentrations of metals in the object, including iron, nickel, cobalt, and chromium, indicated that it had been carved from a meteorite. Further analysis proved that the meteorite was of an extremely rare type known as ataxite, a class of iron meteorites with high nickel content. Astonishingly, its origin could be traced to a specific event in meteorite history. Dr. Buchner and his team discovered that the statue had been carved from a fragment of the Chinga meteorite, which fell in the border areas between Mongolia and Siberia about 15,000 years ago, and was officially discovered in 1913, though there may have been earlier finds from the site. In other words, the 1,000-year-old Buddha statue had an extraterrestrial origin.

However, in October 2012 news broke that there were doubts about the age of the Iron Man (as the statue had become known). Firstly, German historian Isrun Engelhardt, an expert on Schäfer's expedition to Tibet, drew attention to the detailed list that members of the expedition kept of the items they purchased in Tibet. This list, which includes more than 2,000 items, and notes each one's date and place of purchase, as well as its value, makes no mention of a Buddhist statue. Secondly, after examining the statue, Buddhism specialist professor Achim Bayer of the Dongguk University, Seoul, South Korea, identified 13 features of the "lama wearing trousers"[6] as he called it, which he said were obvious proof of fakery. These giveaway features included the full beard, which is not a feature of depictions of Tibetan deities, European-looking shoes rather than boots, trousers instead of robes, the unusual single earring, and a cape more Roman in appearance than ancient Tibetan. Bayer's conclusion was that the "pseudo Tibetan" statue was a European counterfeit made sometime between 1910 and 1970, and was perhaps aimed at the lucrative Nazi memorabilia market. He believed it may have been initially sold with a claimed connection to Schäfer's Tibetan expedition.

However, there are still one or two questions surrounding the statue. Who made it, and how did they obtain such exotic raw material to work on? Furthermore, as the meteorite that the statue was made from is extremely hard and not at all suited to producing sculptures, it has been suggested that rather than being carved, the statue was actually cast by pouring liquid meteoric iron into a mold. Because no reliable documentation of the provenance of the statue has yet been found the origins, whether 20th or 11th century, must remain in doubt, but if it was indeed chiseled from a piece of a meteorite, then it remains the only known example of a human figure carved from such material ever discovered, and as such is an extraordinarily valuable item.

# NOTES

### Introduction
1. "Summary Definition."
2. Bruhns, "International."

### Chapter 2
1. "Tutankhamun: Anatomy."
2. Ibid.
3. Ibid.
4. Ibid.
5. Ibid.
6. Ibid.
7. *New York World,* March 24, 1923.

### Chapter 3
1. Schliemann, *Troy.*
2. Easton, "The Troy."
3. Traill, *Schliemann,*
4. Ibid.
5. Schliemann, *Troy.*

### Chapter 4
1. Herodotus, *The Histories.*
2. Roosevent and Luke, "Looting," pp. 173–187.
3. "Curator Held."
4. *Turkish Daily News,* July 14, 2006.
5. "Karum Piece."
6. Roosevelt and Luke, "Looting."

### Chapter 5
1. Radyuhin, "Massive."
2. Ibid.
3. Conflict Antiquities.

## Chapter 6
1. Singleton, "Plunder."
2. Povoledo, "A Trove."

## Chapter 7
1. Landesman, "The Curse."
2. Riding, "14 Roman."
3. Kennedy, "Not for Sale."
4. Riding, "14 Roman."
5. Fitz Gibbon, *Why?*.
6. Bailey and Ruiz, "The Silver."
7. Ibid.
8. Ibid.

## Chapter 8
1. Guest, *The Late*.
2. Lethbridge, "The Mildenhall."

## Chapter 10
1. Lawson, "Afghan."

## Chapter 11
1. Bede, *Ecclesiastical*.

## Chapter 13
1. Honan, "A Trove."

## Chapter 14
1. "International Cooperation."
2. "Primary Source."

## Chapter 15
1. "Mel's Story."

## Chapter 16
1. Jones, "How."
2. Scott-Clark and Levy, *The Amber Room*.
3. Scott-Clark and Levy, "Secrets."
4. Scott-Clark and Levy, "The Amber Façade."
5. Scott-Clark and Levy, *The Amber Room*.
6. Ibid.
7. Crossland, "Digging."
8. Ibid.

## Chapter 17
1. Brodie, "Persian."
2. Crossland, "Digging."
3. Ibid.
4. Ibid.
5. "Morgan Stanwick AG."
6. Davies, "Nazi."

Adler, Katya. "Looted Libyan treasure 'in Egypt'." BBC News Website, March 11, 2011. *www.bbc.co.uk/news/world-africa-15517886* (accessed 12/28/2012).

Allen, Susan Heuck. "Calvert's Heirs Claim Schliemann Treasure," *Archaeology*, Volume 49, Number 1 (January/February 1996). *www.archaeology.org/9601/newsbriefs/calvert.html* (accessed 12/28/2012).

———. *Finding the Walls of Troy: Frank Calvert and Heinrich Schliemann at Hisarlik*. Berkeley, Calif.: University of California Press, 1999.

Allen, Susan J., and Harry Burton. *Tutankhamun's Tomb: The Thrill of Discovery*. New York: The Metropolitan Museum of Art, 2006.

"Antiquities Missing From Libya." Dorothy King's Phdiva Website, October 31, 2011. *phdiva.blogspot.co.uk/2011/10/antiquities-missing-from-libya.html* (accessed 12/28/2012).

"Archaeological Plunder, Robbery & Vandalism." Temehu Tourism Services Website. *www.temehu.com/Cities_sites/museumvandalism-archaeological-robberies.htm* (accessed 12/28/2012).

"The Archaeological Researches Into Zheng He's Treasure Ships." *Travel China* Website, November 2, 2004. *www.travel-silkroad.com/english/marine/ZhengHe.htm* (accessed 12/28/2012).

"Archaeological Site of Cyrene." UNESCO Website. *whc.unesco.org/en/list/190* (accessed 12/28/2012).

Ashbee, Paul. "Mildenhall: Memories of Mystery and Misgivings." *Antiquity*, Volume 71, Number 271.

B
I
B
L
I
O
G
R
A
P
H
Y

Bailey, Martin. "Interpol Confirms Libyan Treasure Was Looted." *The Art Newspaper,* Issue 229 (November 2011). *www. theartnewspaper.com/articles/Interpol-confirms-Libyan-treasure-was-looted/24900* (accessed 12/28/2012).

Bailey, Martin, and Cristina Ruiz. "The Silver Missing From the Sevso Hoard? And Hungary Wants to Negotiate With Lord Northampton Over Sevso Silver." *Art Law News* Website. *art-law-news.blogspot.co.uk/2007/05/silver-missing-from-sevso-hoard-and.html* (accessed 12/28/2012).

Bard, Kathryn, A. *An Introduction to the Archaeology of Ancient Egypt.* Chicester, UK: John Wiley and Sons Ltd, 2007.

Bede. *Ecclesiastical History of the English People.* Harmondsworth, UK: Penguin Classics, 1990.

Bland, Roger, and Kevin Leahy. *The Staffordshire Hoard.* London: British Museum Press, 2009.

"The Boscoreale Treasure." Louvre Museum Website. *www.louvre.fr/en/oeuvre-notices/boscoreale-treasure* (accessed 12/28/2012).

"Boston University — Central Lydia Archaeological Survey — Looting and Tumulus Reassessment." Boston University Website. *www.bu.edu/clas/activities/heritage-management/looting-and-tumulus-reassessment* (accessed 12/28/2012).

Brodie, Neil. "Persian Mummy." Trafficking Culture Website, August 21, 2012.

*traffickingculture.org/encyclopedia/case-studies/persian-mummy/* (accessed 12/28/2012).

Bromberg, Anne R. *The Quedlinburg Treasury.* Dallas Museum of Art, Texas, 1991.

Bruhns, Karen Olsen. "International Trade in Looted Antiquities." About.com Website. *archaeology.about.com/od/lootingandsmuggling/a/plundered_past.htm* (accessed 12/28/2012).

Burgess, Robert Forrest. *Florida's Golden Galleons — The Search for the 1715 Spanish Treasure Fleet.* Port Solerno, Fla.: Florida Classics Library, 1982.

Campbell, James Graham (ed.). *Viking Treasure from the North West — The Cuerdale Hoard in Context.* Merseyside, UK: National Museums and Galleries, 1992.

Carter, Howard. *The Tomb of Tutankhamun.* New York: Excalibur Books, 1972.

"China to Revive Zheng He's Legend." China.org. *www.china.org.cn/english/culture/180033.htm* (accessed 12/28/2012).

"Collegiate Church, Castle and Old Town of Quedlinburg." UNESCO Website. *whc.unesco.org/en/list/535* (accessed 12/28/2012).

Cooley, Alison E. *Pompeii.* London: Duckworth Archaeological Histories, Bristol Classical Press, 2010.

Covington, Richard. "Lost & Found — Ancient Gold Artifacts From Afghanistan, Hidden for More Than a Decade, Dazzle in a New Exhibition." *Smithsonian* magazine (September 2008). *www.smithsonianmag.com/arts-culture/lost-and-found-afghan.html#ixzz1GjCFIYCG* (accessed 12/28/2012).

Craddock, Paul. *Scientific Investigation of Copies, Fakes and Forgeries.* Oxford, UK: Butterworth-Heinemann Ltd., 2009.

Crossland, David. "Digging for Nazi Treasure: German Treasure Hunters Claim to Have Found Amber Room." *Spiegel* online. *www.spiegel.de/international/germany/digging-for-nazi-treasure-german-treasure-hunters-claim-to-have-found-amber-room-a-536358.html* (accessed 12/28/2012).

"Curator Held on Croesus's Stolen Riches." Suna Erdem. *Times,* May 30, 2006. *www.thetimes.co.uk/tto/arts/article2406262.ece*

Dahl, R. *The Mildenhall Treasure.* London: Jonathan Cape, 1999.

Davies, Lizzy. "Nazi Buddha From Space Might Be Fake." *The Guardian* online, October 24, 2012. *www.guardian.co.uk/science/2012/oct/24/nazi-buddha-statue-space-fake* (accessed 12/28/2012).

Doole, Jenny. "The Mystery of the Persian Mummy," *Culture Without Context* (Autumn 2001) 9: 14–15. Website of the Illicit Antiquities Research Centre, at the McDonald Institute for Archaeological Research at the University of Cambridge. *www.mcdonald.cam.ac.uk/projects/iarc/culturewithoutcontext/issue9/doole-review.htm* (accessed 12/28/2012).

Dreyer, Edward L. *Zheng He: China and the Oceans in the Early Ming Dynasty, 1405–1433.* New York: Pearson Longman, 2007.

Dunn, Jimmy. "Egypt: Tutankhamun (King Tut) of the 18th Dynasty." Tour Egypt Website. *www.touregypt.net/featurestories/tut.htm* (accessed 12/28/2012).

Easton, D.F. "The Troy Treasures in Russia." *Antiquity*, Vol. 69, No. 262 (March 1995).

Edsel, Robert M. *The Monuments Men: Allied Heroes, Nazi Thieves and the Greatest Treasure Hunt in History.* Brentwood, Tenn.: Center Street, 2010.

Erlanger, Steven. "Digging Out Schliemann's Treasure at the Pushkin." *New York Times,* December 11, 1994. *www.nytimes. com/1994/12/11/arts/art-digging-out-schliemann-s-treasure-at-the-pushkin.html?pagewanted=all&src=pm* (accessed 12/28/2012).

"Facts and Figures." Saving Antiquities for Everyone Website. *www. savingantiquities.org/about/facts-figures/* (accessed 12/28/2012).

Fagan, Brian M., Neil Asher Silberman, and Charlotte Beck (eds.). *The Oxford Companion to Archaeology.* New York: Oxford University Press, 1996.

Felch, Jason, and Ralph Frammolino. *Chasing Aphrodite: the Hunt for Looted Antiquities at the World's Richest Museum.* Boston, Mass.: Houghton Mifflin Harcourt, 2011.

"Fighting Illegal International Trade in Cultural Artifacts." University of Glasgow College of Social Sciences Website. *www.gla.ac.uk/colleges/socialsciences/research/features/ crimeandjusticetradeinculturalartefacts/* (accessed 12/28/2012).

Fine, John Christopher. *Treasures of the Spanish Main: Shipwrecked Galleons in the New World.* Guilford, Conn.: Lyons Press, 2006.

Fitz Gibbon, Kate (ed). *Who Owns the Past?: Cultural Policy, Cultural Property, and the Law.* New Jersey: Rutgers University Press, 2005.

Foss, Pedar. *The World of Pompeii.* Florency, Ky.: Routledge, 2008.

George, Rose. "The Great Smash and Grab." *The Independent* online, January 5, 2005. *www.independent.co.uk/news/world/europe/the-great-smash-and-grab-6147004.html* (accessed 12/28/2012).

Gould, Dr. Richard. "Asia's Undersea Archeology." PBS Website. *www.pbs.org/wgbh/nova/sultan/archeology2.html* (accessed 12/28/2012).

Graham-Campbell, James, and Gareth Williams (eds). *Silver Economy in the Viking Age.* Walnut Creek, Calif.: Left Coast Press, 2007.

Grinsell, Leslie V. *Folklore of Prehistoric Sites in Britain.* Devon, UK: David and Charles, 1976.

Guest, Peter S.W. *The Late Roman Gold and Silver Coins From the Hoxne Treasure.* London: British Museum Press, 2005.

Gunde, Richard. "Zheng He's Voyages of Discovery." UCLA Asia Institute Website. *www.international.ucla.edu/asia/news/article. asp?parentid=10387* (accessed 12/28/2012).

Hadingham, Evan. "Ancient Chinese Explorers." PBS Website. *www.pbs.org/wgbh/nova/ancient/ancient-chinese-explorers.html* (accessed 12/28/2012).

Harris J. E., and F. Hussien F. "The Identification of the Eighteenth Dynasty Royal Mummies: A Biological Perspective," *International Journal of Osteoarchaeology* 1 (1991): 235–239.

Hawass, Zahi A. *Tutankhamun and the Golden Age of the Pharaohs.* Washington, D.C.: National Geographic Society, 2005.

Hawley, Caroline. "Libya's Historic Treasures Survive the Revolution." BBC News Website, March 11, 2011. *www.bbc. co.uk/news/world-middle-east-15557403* (accessed 12/28/2012).

Herodotus. *The Histories.* Harmondsworth, UK: Penguin Books, 1996.

Hickley, Catherine. "Stasi's Secret Quest for Czar's Amber Room Cost Millions." *Businessweek* Website. March 27, 2012. *www. businessweek.com/news/2012-03-27/stasi-s-secret-quest-for-czar-s-lost-amber-room-cost-millions* (accessed 12/28/2012).

Hiebert, Fredrik, and Pierre Cambon. *Afghanistan: Hidden Treasures From the National Museum, Kabul.* Washington, D.C.: National Geographic, 2008.

"Hoards and Hoarding." *Current Archaeology* (October 1, 2010). *www. archaeology.co.uk/articles/news/hoards-and-hoarding.htm* (accessed 12/28/12).

Hobbs, Richard. "The Secret History of the Mildenhall Treasure." *Antiquaries Journal* 88: 376–420.

———. *Treasure: Finding our Past.* London: The British Museum Press, 2003.

Honan, William H. *Treasure Hunt – A New York Times Reporter Tracks the Quedlinburg Hoard.* New York: Fromm International, 1997.

———. "A Trove of Medieval Art Turns Up in Texas." *New York Times,* June 14, 1990. *www.nytimes.com/1990/06/14/arts/a-trove-of-medieval-art-turns-up-in-texas.html?pagewanted=all&src=pm* (accessed 12/28/2012).

Horner, D. *The Treasure Galleons.* New York: Dodd, Mead, and Co., 1971.

"The Hoxne Hoard." British Museum Website. *www.britishmuseum. org/explore/highlights/highlight_objects/pe_prb/t/the_hoxne_hoard. aspx* (accessed 12/28/2012).

"Hoxne Hoard." *Current Archaeology* Website, October 1, 2010. *http://www.archaeology.co.uk/articles/news/hoxne.htm* (accessed 12/28/2012).

"The Hoxne Hoard." Hoxne.net. *www.hoxne.net/history/hoard.html* (accessed 12/28/2012).

"The Influence of the Occult on the 1939 German Expedition to Tibet." Tibet Talk blog, December 24, 2009. *tibettalk.wordpress. com/2009/12/24/the-influence-of-the-occult-on-the-1939-german-expedition-to-tibet/#more-835* (accessed 12/28/2012).

"International Cooperation Agreement on Malacca Strait Safety." *The Maritime Executive,* April 2, 2008. *www.maritime-executive. com/article/2007-09-13international-cooperation-agreement-on/* (accessed 12/28/2012).

Jackson, Brittany, and Mark Rose. "Archaeology's Hoaxes, Fakes, and Strange Sites – Saitaphernes' Golden Tiara." *Archaeology* magazine Website. *www.archaeology.org/online/features/hoaxes/ saitaphernes_tiara.html* (accessed 12/28/2012).

Johns, Catherine. *The Hoxne Late Roman Treasure: Gold Jewelry and Silver Plate.* London: British Museum Press, 2010.

Jones, Alex. "The Staffordshire Hoard Fieldwork, 2009–2010." Papers from the Staffordshire Hoard Symposium. Portable Antiquities Scheme Website. *finds.org.uk/staffshoardsymposium/ papers/alexjones* (accessed 12/28/2012).

Jones, Lewis. "How the World's Eighth Wonder Was Lost in Transit." *The Telegraph,* June 13, 2004. *www.telegraph.co.uk/culture/ books/3618885/How-the-worlds-eighth-wonder-was-lost-in-transit. html* (accessed 12/28/2012).

"Karun piece found in Germany." *Hurriyet Daily News* Website, November 22, 2012. *www. hurriyetdailynews.com/karun-piece-found-in-germany. aspx?pageID=238&nID=35155&NewsCatID=375* (accessed 12/28/2012).

Kaye, Lawrence M., and Carla T. Main. "The Saga of the Lydian Hoard Antiquities: From Uşak to New York and Back and Some Related Observations on the Law of Cultural Repatriation." In Kathryn W. Tubb (ed.), *Antiquities, Trade or Betrayed. Legal, Ethical and Conservation Issues.* London: Archetype, 1995, pp. 150–162.

Kennedy, Maev. "Evidence for Unknown Viking king Airdeconut Found in Lancashire." *The Guardian* Website, December 14, 2011. *www.guardian.co.uk/science/2011/dec/14/viking-king-airdeconut-treasure-lancashire* (accessed 12/28/2012).

———. "Largest Ever Hoard of Anglo-Saxon Gold Found in Staffordshire." *The Guardian* Website, September 24, 2009. *www.guardian.co.uk/uk/2009/sep/24/anglo-saxon-treasure-hoard-gold-staffordshire-metal-detector* (accessed 12/28/2012).

———. "Not for Sale Yet—the 'Cursed' 14 Pieces of Silver Worth £100m." *The Guardian* Website, October 17, 2006. *www. guardian.co.uk/uk/2006/oct/17/arts.artsnews* (Accessed 12/28/2012).

"King Tut's Curse!" *Skeptoid* #106 (June 24, 2008). *skeptoid.com/ episodes/4106* (accessed 12/28/2012).

Kruse, Susan E. "Ingots and Weight Units in Viking Age Silver Hoards." *World Archaeology* 20(2) (1998): 285–301.

Kuttner, Ann L. *Dynasty and Empire in the Age of Augustus: The Case of the Boscoreale Cups.* Berkeley, Calif.: University of California Press, 1995.

Lamm, Jan Peder. "Two Large Silver Hoards from Ocksarve on Gotland. Evidence for Viking Period Trade and Warfare in the Baltic Region." My Eclectic Page Website. *mycoinpage.com/SCA/ ArmRings/SilverHoardsFromGotland.pdf* (accessed 12/28/2012).

Landesman, Peter. "The Curse of the Sevso Treasure." *Atlantic Magazine* (November 2001). *www.theatlantic.com/magazine/ archive/2001/11/the-curse-of-the-sevso-silver/302331/* (accessed 12/28/2012).

"Last Chance to See the Viking Hoard." Yorkshire Museum Website. *www.yorkshiremuseum.org.uk/Page/ViewNewsArticle. aspx?ArticleId=22* (accessed 12/28/2012).

Lawler, Andrew. "Claims of Mass Libyan Looting Rejected by Archaeologists." The American Association for the Advancement of Science Website, September 1, 2011. *news. sciencemag.org/scienceinsider/2011/09/claims-of-mass-libyan-looting.html* (accessed 12/28/2012).

Lawson, Alastair. "Afghan Gold: How the Country's Heritage Was Saved." BBC News Website, March 1, 2011. *www.bbc.co.uk/ news/world-south-asia-12599726* (accessed 12/28/2012).

Leahy, Kevin. "The Contents of the Hoard." Papers from the Staffordshire Hoard Symposium. Portable Antiquities Scheme Website. *finds.org.uk/staffshoardsymposium/papers/kevinleahy* (accessed 12/28/2012).

Lethbridge, T.C. "The Mildenhall Treasure: A First-Hand Account." *Antiquity* Vol. 71, No. 273 (September 1997).

Levathes, Louise. *When China Ruled the Seas: The Treasure Fleet of the Dragon Throne, 1405–1433.* New York: Oxford University Press, 1996.

Marchant, Jo. "Tutankhamun—the Secrets of the Tomb Go Online." *The Guardian* Website. *www.guardian.co.uk/culture/2010/jul/18/ tutankhamun-website-howard-carter-tomb* (accessed 12/28/2012).

Massie, Robert K. *Catherine the Great: Portrait of a Woman.* Mississauga, Ont., Canada: Random House of Canada, Limited, 2011.

McDonnell, Ronan. "Chiemsee." *The Inquisition* Website, September 18th, 2009. *theinquisition.eu/wordpress/2009/history/chiemsee/* (accessed 12/28/2012).

McGrath, Matt. "Ancient Statue Discovered by Nazis Is Made From Meteorite." BBC News Website, September 27, 2012. *www.bbc. co.uk/news/science-environment-19735959* (accessed 12/28/2012).

The Mel Fisher Maritime Museum Website. *www.melfisher.org/index. htm* (accessed 12/28/2012).

"The Mildenhall Treasure." Mildenhall Museum Website. *www. mildenhallmuseum.co.uk/Treasure.htm* (accessed 12/28/2012).

Moorehead, Caroline. *Lost and Found: Heinrich Schliemann and the Gold That Got Away.* E. Rutherford, N.J.: Penguin (Non-Classics), 1997.

"Morgan Stanwick AG." Moneyhouse Website. *www.moneyhouse.ch/en/u/morgan_stanwick_ag_CH-320.3.057.559-6.htm* (accessed 12/28/2012).

Morganitina—The American Excavations home page. *morgantina.org/* (accessed 12/28/2012).

Mundell Mango, Marlia, and Anna Bennett. "The Sevso Treasure - Art Historical Description and Inscriptions, and Methods of Manufacture and Scientific Analyses," *Journal of Roman Archaeology Supplementary Series* (1993) no.12.1.

Nalley, Richard. "Mysteries of the Amber Room." *Forbes Magazine,* March 29, 2004. *www.forbes.com/forbes-life-magazine/2004/0329/048.html* (accessed 12/28/2012).

"New Mystery Surrounds Treasure." BBC News Website, January 7, 2003. *news.bbc.co.uk/1/hi/england/2635239.stm* (accessed 12/28/2012).

Nicholas, Lynn H. *The Rape of Europa: The Fate of Europe's Treasures in the Third Reich and the Second World War.* New York: Vintage Books, 1995.

Osborn, Andrew. "Top Russian Spy's Body Washes up 'After Swimming Accident'." *The Telegraph* online, October 31, 2010. *www.telegraph.co.uk/news/worldnews/europe/russia/7973346/Top-Russian-spys-body-washes-up-after-swimming-accident.html* (accessed 12/28/2012).

Owen, James. "Huge Viking Hoard Discovered in Sweden." *National Geographic News* Website, April 8, 2008. *news.nationalgeographic.com/news/2008/04/080408-viking-hoard.html* (accessed 12/28/2012).

Özgen, I., and J. Öztürk. *The Lydian Treasure: Heritage Recovered.* Istanbul, Republic of Turkey: Ministry of Culture General Directorate of Monuments and Museums, 1996.

Painter, K.S. *The Mildenhall Treasure, Roman Silver From East Anglia.* London: British Museum Press, 1977.

Painter, Kenneth S. *The Insula of the Menander at Pompeii — Volume IV: The Silver Treasure.* New York: Oxford University Press, 2002.

Parsons, Marie. "Royal Caches at Deir el-Bahri." TourEgpyt.net. *www. touregypt.net/featurestories/cache.htm* (accessed 12/28/2012).

Partridge, Bob. "Finding Tutankhamun." *World Archaeology,* Issue 36 (July 3, 2009). *www.world-archaeology.com/world/africa/egypt/ finding-tutankhamun/* (accessed 12/28/2012).

Povoledo, Elizabetta. "A Trove of Ancient Silver Said to Be Stolen Returns to its Home in Sicily." *New York Times* online, December 5, 2010. *www.nytimes.com/2010/12/06/ arts/design/06silver.html?pagewanted=all&_r=0* (accessed 12/28/2012).

"Primary Source – Zheng He's Inscription." University of Minnesota, Deptartment of History Website. *www.hist.umn.edu/hist1012/ primarysource/source.htm* (accessed 12/28/2012).

Radyuhin, Vladimir. "Massive Looting of Ancient Artefacts Underway in Libya." *The Hindu* online, August 28, 2011. *www.thehindu.com/opinion/op-ed/article2409474.ece* (accessed 12/28/2012).

Reeves, Nicholas. *The Complete Tutankhamun: The King, The Tomb, The Royal Treasure.* London: Thames & Hudson, 1994.

Riding, Alan. "14 Roman Treasures, on View and Debated." *New York Times,* October 26, 2006. *www.nytimes.com/2006/10/25/arts/ design/25sevs.html?pagewanted=1&;usco* (accessed 12/28/2012).

Röbel, Sven. "The Mystery of the 'Nazi Holy Grail'." *Spiegel* online, April 23, 2007. *www.spiegel.de/international/spiegel/treasure- hunters-art-dealers-and-swindlers-the-mystery-of-the-nazi-holy- grail-a-478958.html* (accessed 12/28/2012).

Romey, Kristin M., and Mark Rose. "Special Report: Saga of the Persian Princess." *Archaeology* Volume 54 Number 1 (January/ February 2001). *Archaeology* magazine Website. *www. archaeology.org/0101/etc/persia.html* (accessed 12/28/2012).

Roosevelt, C.H., and C. Luke. "Looting Lydia: The Destruction of an Archaeological Landscape in Western Turkey." In *Archaeology, Cultural Heritage, and the Antiquities Trade,* edited by N. Brodie, M.M. Kersel, C. Luke, and K.W. Tubb. Gainesville, Fla.: University Press of Florida, 2006, pp. 173–87.

Rose, Mark. "The Staffordshire Hoard Appeal." *Archaeology* magazine Website, January 24, 2010. *archaeology.org/blog/?p=851* (accessed 12/28/2012).

Samarkeolog. "Libya: Looting Claims Rejected; Propaganda Accusations Not Denied." *conflict Antiquities* Website. *conflictantiquities.wordpress.com/2011/09/03/libya-looting-propaganda-2/* (accessed 12/28/2012).

Sarianidi, V.I. "The Treasure of Golden Hill." *American Journal of Archaeology* Vol. 84, No. 2 (April 1980): 125–31.

Sarianidi, Victor. "Tillya Tepe: The Burial of a Noble Warrior." *PERSICA* XIV (1990–1992): 103–130.

Schliemann, Heinrich. *Troy and its Remains: A Narrative of Researches and Discoveries Made on the Site of Ilium, and in the Trojan Plain.* Cambridge, UK: Cambridge Library Collection — Archaeology, 2010.

Schuller, Sepp. *Forgers, Dealers, Experts: Strange Chapters in Art History.* New York: G.P. Putnam's Sons, 1960.

Scott-Clark, Catherine, and Adrian Levy. "The Amber Façade." *The Guardian* (May 22, 2004). *www.guardian.co.uk/artanddesign/2004/may/22/art.russia* (accessed 12/28/2012).

———. *The Amber Room: The Untold Story of the Greatest Hoax of the Twentieth Century.* London: Atlantic Books, 2004.

———. Secrets and Lies Website. *www.secrets-and-lies.co.uk/books-2/the-amber-room/the-amber-room-more-reviews/* (accessed 12/28/2012).

"Sevso Treasure." BBC Website. *www.bbc.co.uk/insideout/east/series11/week9_castle_ashby.shtml* (accessed 12/28/2012).

Shaw, Ian. *The Oxford History of Ancient Egypt.* New York: Oxford University Press, 2004.

"Shipping News: Zheng He's Sexcentenary." *China Heritage Newsletter* Website. *chinaheritagenewsletter.anu.edu.au/articles.php?searchterm=002_zhenghe.inc&issue=002* (accessed 12/28/2012).

Singleton, Maura. "Plunder — The Theft of the Morgantina Silver." *University of Virginia Magazine* (Spring 2006). *archives.uvamagazine.org/site/c.esJNK1PIJrH/b.1601299/k.E0D/Plunder_The_theft_of_the_Morgantina_silver.htm* (accessed 12/28/2012).

Sox, David. *Unmasking the Forger, the Dossena Deception.* New York: Universe Books, 1987.

"Staffordshire Hoard." Birmingham Museum and Art Gallery Website. *www.bmag.org.uk/collections/staffordshire-hoard* (accessed 12/28/2012).

Staffordshire Hoard Website. *www.staffordshirehoard.org.uk/.*

"Summary Definition of Treasure." Portable Antiquities Scheme Website. *finds.org.uk/treasure/advice/summary* (accessed 12/28/12).

Sutton Hoo Society Website. *www.suttonhoo.org/index.asp* (Accessed 12/28/2012).

Thomas, Suzie. "Morgantina Silver." Trafficking Culture Website. *traffickingculture.org/encyclopedia/case-studies/morgantina-silver/* (accessed 12/28/2012).

Thurborg, Marit. "Regional Economic Structures: An Analysis of the Viking Age Silver Hoards from Oland, Sweden." *World Archaeology* 20(2) )1988): 302–24.

Tolstikov, Vladimir, and Michail Yu Treister. *The Gold of Troy: Searching for Homer's Fabled City.* New York: Harry N. Abrams, 1996.

Traill, David. *Schliemann of Troy: Treasure and Deceit.* Gordonsville, Va.: St. Martin's Press, 1997.

"Treasure Act 1996." The National Archives HM Government UK legislation Website. *www.legislation.gov.uk/ukpga/1996/24/contents* (accessed 12/28/2012).

"Treasure of Benghazi Stolen in One of the Biggest Heists in Archaeological History." Fox News Website, October 30, 2011. *www.foxnews.com/world/2011/10/30/treasure-benghazi-stolen-in-one-biggest-heists-in-archaeological-history/* (accessed 12/28/2012).

"A Treasure Hunt — The Case of Afghanistan's Missing Cache." *The Economist* online, December 18, 2003. *www.economist.com/node/2281950* (accessed 12/28/2012).

"Trophies of Kings: The Staffordshire Hoard." *Current Archaeology* Website, September 30, 2009. *www.archaeology.co.uk/articles/features/trophies-of-kings-the-staffordshire-hoard.htm* (accessed 12/28/2012).

"Tutankhamun: Anatomy of an Excavation." The Griffith Institute Website. *www.griffith.ox.ac.uk/tutankhamundiscovery.html* (accessed 12/28/2012).

Tyldesley Joyce, A. *Hatchepsut: The Female Pharaoh.* New York: Penguin (Non-Classics), 1998.

Walton, Timothy R. *The Spanish Treasure Fleets.* Sarasota, Fla.: Pineapple Press, 1994.

Watson, Peter, and Cecelia Todeschini. *The Medici Conspiracy: The Illicit Journey of Looted Antiquities – From Italy's Tomb Raiders to the World's Greatest Museums.* New York: PublicAffairs, 2007.

Waxman, Sharon. *Loot: The Battle Over the Stolen Treasures of the Ancient World.* New York: Times Books, 2009.

Westwood, Jennifer, and Jacqueline Simpson. *The Lore of the Land: A Guide to England's Legends, From Spring-Heeled Jack to the Witches of Warboys.* London: Penguin, 2005.

Wilford, John Noble. "Archeologists Rally to Defense of Flawed Giant." *New York Times,* January 16, 1996. *www.nytimes. com/1996/01/16/science/archeologists-rally-to-defense-of-flawed-giant.html?pagewanted=all&src=pm* (accessed 12/28/2012).

Williams, Gareth, and Leslie Webster. "The Cuerdale Hoard." BBC History Website. *www.bbc.co.uk/history/ancient/vikings/cuerdale_01.shtml* (accessed 12/28/2012).

Yates, Donna. "Benghazi Treasure." *Trafficking Culture* Website, December 9, 2012. *traffickingculture.org/encyclopedia/case-studies/benghazi-treasure/* (accessed 12/28/2012).

Zaluckyj, Sarah. *Mercia: The Anglo-Saxon Kingdom of Central England.* Almeley, Herefordshire, UK: Logaston Press, 2011.

# INDEX

# ABOUT THE AUTHOR

*A* qualified archaeologist, BRIAN HAUGHTON is an author and researcher on the subjects of prehistoric megalithic sites, ancient sacred places, and supernatural folklore.

Haughton's first book, *Hidden History: Lost Civilizations, Secret Knowledge, and Ancient Mysteries*, was published in January 2007 and has been translated into 11 languages, including German, Russian, Greek, and Thai. This was followed by *Haunted Spaces, Sacred Places; The Lore of the Ghost;* and *History's Mysteries.* This title will be his fifth book with New Page Books.

Brian's work has been featured in various print publications across the world, including *Doorways Magazine, Awareness,* and *All Destiny,* and on Websites such as the BBC's Legacies, World Mysteries, and the Book of Thoth. He is a member of the Folklore Society (England) and serves as a consultant for the UK-based research and investigative organization Parasearch. He long ago fell for the lure of the ancient world and tales of the supernatural, initially inspired by visiting the Neolithic chambered tombs of the Cotswold Hills in England and by reading the ghost stories of Sheridan Le Fanu and M.R. James.

In his spare time Brian plays synthesizer in the band the Star Fields.